I, LUCIFER

Exploring the Archetype and Origins of the Devil

Corvis Nocturnum

Exploring the Archetype and Origins of the Devil

I. LUCIFER

Other Schiffer Books By The Author:
Cemetery Gates: Death and Mourning Through the Ages
ISBN 978-0-7643-3787-1, Price: $24.99

Text and images by author unless otherwise noted

Schiffer Books are available at special discounts for bulk purchases for sales promotions or premiums. Special editions, including personalized covers, corporate imprints, and excerpts can be created in large quantities for special needs. For more information contact the publisher:

Published by Schiffer Publishing Ltd.
4880 Lower Valley Road
Atglen, PA 19310
Phone: (610) 593-1777; Fax: (610) 593-2002
E-mail: Info@schifferbooks.com

For the largest selection of fine reference books on this and related subjects, please visit our website at
www.schifferbooks.com
We are always looking for people to write books on new and related subjects. If you have an idea for a book, please contact us at
proposals@schifferbooks.com

Title Page:
Dore's *Satan trapped in Hell 1887.*
Courtesy of Library of Congress.

This book may be purchased from the publisher.
Include $5.00 for shipping.
Please try your bookstore first.
You may write for a free catalog.

In Europe, Schiffer books are distributed by
Bushwood Books
6 Marksbury Ave.
Kew Gardens
Surrey TW9 4JF England
Phone: 44 (0) 20 8392 8585; Fax: 44 (0) 20 8392 9876
E-mail: info@bushwoodbooks.co.uk
Website: www.bushwoodbooks.co.uk

Designed by RoS
Type set in Formal436 BT/NewBskvll BT

ISBN: 978-0-7643-3919-6
Printed in China

Dedication

This book is dedicated to the free thinkers and open minded people of all faiths and walks of life that have given me the chance to share my work with them and, in turn, explain their world view.

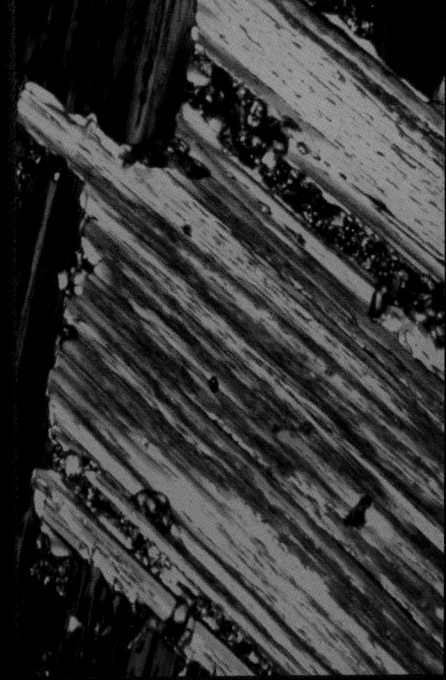

Acknowledgements

Special thanks to the following people, without whom this would not have been possible:

Hyde Brother's Books, Michelle Belanger (for her ideas and use of her vast personal library, thank you!), Magus Anton Szandor LaVey, Magus Peter H. Gilmore, Magister Paradise, Magister Johnson, Kevin I. Slaughter, Scarlet Norton of Diabolic Publications, Priestess Helena of Dark Candle Company, Warlock Les Hernandez, Warlock Jason Leach, Storm Anderson, Reverend Gavin Baddeley, Professor Kevin Eads, Michael Moynihan, Dante Alighieri, John Milton, Gustave Dore, William Blake, The Rolling Stones, Al Pacino, Marilyn Mansfeild, Timothy Ringenberg, Magister Sass, Magister Frost, Kenneth V. Lanning, my editor, Dinah Roseberry, and Mr. Schiffer.

And to Starr, Jack, and Michelle for helping me make Dark Moon Press what it has become.

CONTENTS

Introduction

Lucifer by Liege Luc Viatour, Cathedral of St. Paul, Liège, Belgium. *Courtesy Library of Congress.*

> *"Please allow me to introduce myself; I'm a man of wealth and taste."*
> ~ Rolling Stones

Lucifer. The Devil. Satan. The many names that the accuser has been known by over the centuries has both been feared by and, in some cases, glorified by others.

I. Lucifer: Exploring the Archetype and Origins of the Devil examines the many aspects of this evolving archetype, from his multifaceted creation within many countries and faiths, to his almost endearing charm on today's world stage. As superstitions gave way to religion for answers on the unexplainable fear of the things that go bump in the night, humanity turned to science and philosophy that more clearly exposed the irrational for what it was. Although we would like to believe we as a human race have evolved away from myths and superstitions, we retain the core ideas of what is good and what is evil. Such concepts may appear at first thought as simple and clear, but when asked to define it exactly, the waters get muddy. We learn right and wrong during childhood from the adults around us. As children, we question what we are told with the innocent "why?" but was that the fatal flaw originally? ...Questioning the maker's dictations, not the first transgression of the Devil himself? Perhaps man is truly born in sin as some theologians insist, into a world of evils, that our fate is to suffer until death frees us from our plight. Or is it all a large hoax, perpetrated by those who would stop at nothing to hide the truth, that we are the sole cause of our own misfortunes, by poor choices.

I. Lucifer challenges the idea that the Devil is a real being, and offers the alternative notion that he is merely an archetype that has evolved from our collective unconscious, developed and reshaped constantly from borrowed ideas and given strength by sheer numbers of believers. We'll explore myths and legends of Satan, as this work seeks to explore the opposing sides in what Lucifer represents in our culture and the effects it has had over the centuries. From dogmatic repression of pagan beliefs during witch trials in the days of the *Malleus Maleficarum*, which caused a series of counter actions by the Black Metal "Devil Worshippers" and the fervor during the heights of the "Satanic Panic" of the 1980s and 1990s. We'll examine the front-line defense at the forefront of old Nicks case from Anton LaVey's Church of Satan, as well as on up to literature and films that played a role in redefining this ever-evolving archetype.

I ask you to join me in learning the aspects of his origins, and see from what other faiths have been borrowed to shape our mental picture of the being known as The Devil. In the spirit of the great accuser, the adversary, I take the side of the Devil's advocate asking my readers to suspend preconceived notions, and follow me into the past for a look at this mythic personas origin up to his modern day evolution!

~ Corvis Nocturnum

Chapter One

The Long Fall from Grace

Dieric Bouts the Elder 1450. *The Fall of the Damned Uzi Dornai.*

The Devil has remained among the most popular of all iconic figures of human civilization for centuries; to be clear, Satan has far from exhausted his charming appeal – to see it, one only need to browse thousands upon thousands of libraries, bookstores, and the Internet for literally millions of entries. We see proof of this even more so as Satan as an archetype reigns second to none in the popular character imagination in a multitude of films featuring the Devil himself, with the masterful portrayals of Jack Nicholson, in *The Witches of Eastwick*, and especially my personal favorite, Al Pacino in *The Devil's Advocate*. Classics like *Rosemary's Baby* and *The Omen* are still watched, and the Devil makes his presence known in cartoons like *South Park*, and in many comic books and of course throughout the entire history of rock and roll.

Fall of Lucifer, Gustave Doré's 1866 illustration for *Paradise Lost* by John Milton.

This book goes into numerous examples from widely divergent cultures that share in the evolution of most prominent characteristics – and proves this concept of a persona of the Devil is far from sole property of Christianity, indeed "his presence" is known throughout history, regardless of the time and place. Satan is simply a crystallization of these forms into a single being.

The subject of the Devil may be approached in many different ways, including historical, theological, and psychological. It is my intention to examine the topic as a manifestation of the mind, both individually in all of us by way of how we perceive him, and collectively showing how we have shaped the idea of what or whom the Devil is. My approach is not intended to be confrontational to the religious follower of any Judeo-Christian faith; rather I seek to provide a interpretation of the social context in relation to our world view as a whole. My study is based on historical information regarding the mythology of the Devil, in an open-minded fashion without disrespect. Theologians cannot obtain what is known as empirical knowledge when speaking of anything pertaining to the Devil. Empirical knowledge is found only in the observation of events, and the only "evil" that occurs are the actions man physically participates, and must be judged solely by. What we are left with then is a historical and folkloric representation that has always been in fluid motion, a malleable and easily twisted concept to take on the form of whatever the egalitarian society that controls it wishes it to appear. Religious truth is not absolute; it is subjective at best. Evil has long been personified as a sentient being, far before the writing of the New Testament. Manifestations of a Devil have been a part of man since prehistoric times, and due to the need of the frail human psyche to shift our fear reaction onto a living breathing source, or to a scapegoat for our own worst personal thoughts and actions, and as such, there will always be a "Devil" in our midst. From a philosophical perspective, the universal belief in evil demons is based on the need for an explanation of the enormous real quantity of moral and physical evil pervading human existence for our entire history.

The Lucifer Archetype

As time went on, people slowly began to be seen as things which existed solely within a person's mind, rather than a complex supernatural figure in our world. During the 1850s, Sigmund Freud argued that religion was "a symptom of psychological and emotional alienation from oneself and family, rather than any deity." In Freud's perception, the idea of the Devil said more about us, than it did about any existing literal entities. What we project, think (manifest), and do to one another is "Lucifer's reality." In psychological terms, an archetype can be broadly described as a model of a type of person or behavior that can be used in an interpretive manner behavior; they can be further divided into two sub-categories. First, in regards to stereotypes, which refer to one type of personality or behavior being observed many times, also epitomes a certain personality or behavior.

To draw the relationship between psychology and religion, two theories need to be examined. The first is the existence of the unconscious; a part of the human psyche controls our consciousness, as witnessed by example by way of Freudian slips. The second assumption is the direct relationship between the individual and that of the collective society. Society is composed of individuals as a collective in Jungian terms, and individuals are created by society, so collectively over the span of time humanity we thus *create archetypes from our subconscious fears*. We ourselves indirectly created the figure that became the Devil – or by whatever name was most appropriate for the particular period or culture one finds them in happens to call that archetype.

Awareness of archetypes dates back as far as Plato, who called them "Forms." Plato believed that these

Forms were reflected in material objects. For Jung, archetypes comprised psychological patterns that came from classic roles around us. Jung asserted, "...there exists a second psychic system of a collective, universal, and impersonal nature that is identical in all individuals... The archetypes are both linked to the instincts and to spirituality... (and) existed from the earliest record of human history," and can be found in plays ranging from Shakespeare to modern cinematic classics. We see this time and time again, typically the figures are larger-than-life, indeed in all fiction from ancient myths of Greece to the *Star Wars* Obi Wan Kenobi as the hermit (or the magician), we see as Gandalf in *The Lord of The Rings*, Casanova as the lover, and of course the Devil or trickster. Mythology is best understood in terms of metaphors, and as Jung says, "Man makes his idea of God in his own image. God and Satan are merely projections, human

Carl Jung. *Photo courtesy Library of Congress.*

ideas they project. Although the many different ancient religions had different Gods with different personalities and different names, they are aspects of ourselves, key roles that exist within all of us." Lucifer represented self-knowledge, and this fallen angel became a powerful force that threatened the Church's ability to control the masses as pagan gods were warped into demons by the Middle Ages. As we will see, the archetype evolved further in chapters to come; we will discover Lucifer is just a name that belongs to the thought "Form" that we have been taught to fear, an archetypal avatar of knowledge and defiance.

People need to identify these spirits in different ways to understand them. This concept is enhanced as other similar deities/archetypes as Jean Shinoda Bolen, in her book, *Gods In Everyman*, talks about the Greek gods as male archetypes. The ancient gods and demigods of many cultures saw Hercules as the hero archetype, for example.

All myths, all gods are archetypal, merely representing thought-patterns, believe many psychologists and writers such as Joseph Campbell, who lived from March 26, 1904 to October 30, 1987. He was famous as an American mythologist, writer, and lecturer, and best known for his work in comparative mythology and religion. His name might be familiar as he appeared before his death on The History Channel, talking about *Star Wars* in Jungian terms. I studied much of his work myself after realizing he wrote introductions to Nietzsche's translated works. Campbell's theory is that when we simplify traits of people or powerful emotions, it becomes clearer to us how the ancient Greek and Romans thought and translated this theory into more anthropomorphized beings so they could understand them in basic human terms. Aphrodite, the goddess of beauty and lust, Mars was the personification of aggression; Prometheus (as well as the Nordic trickster god Loki) share the aspect of rebellion to dogma and the triumph of man to evolve as I wrote in detail on the major groups and individuals in my work *Promethean Flame* back in 2007.

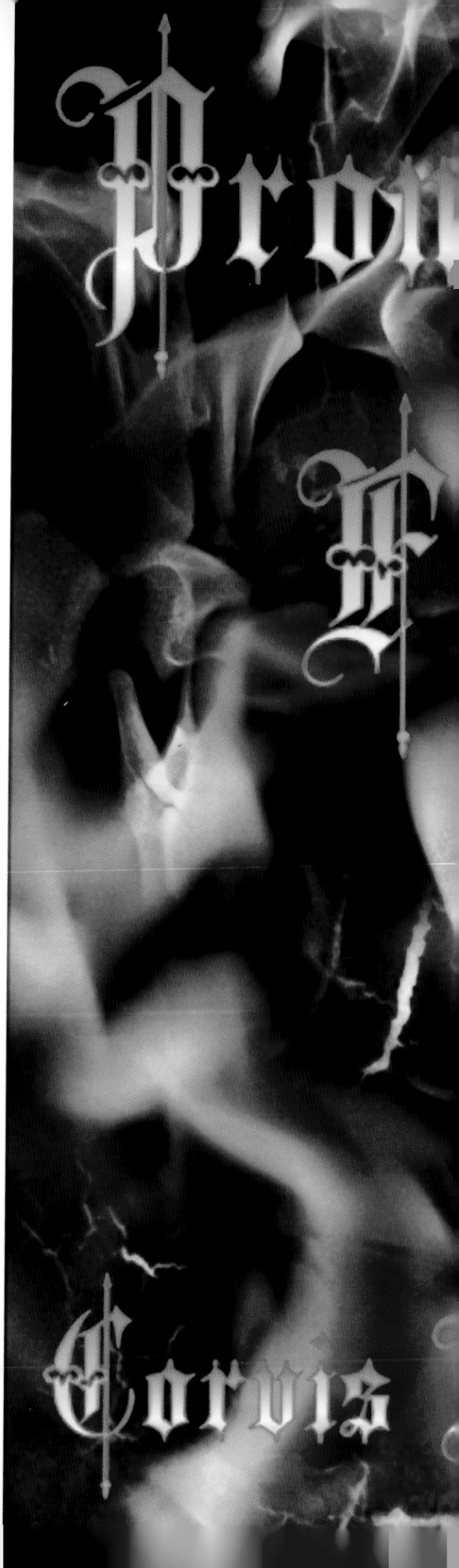

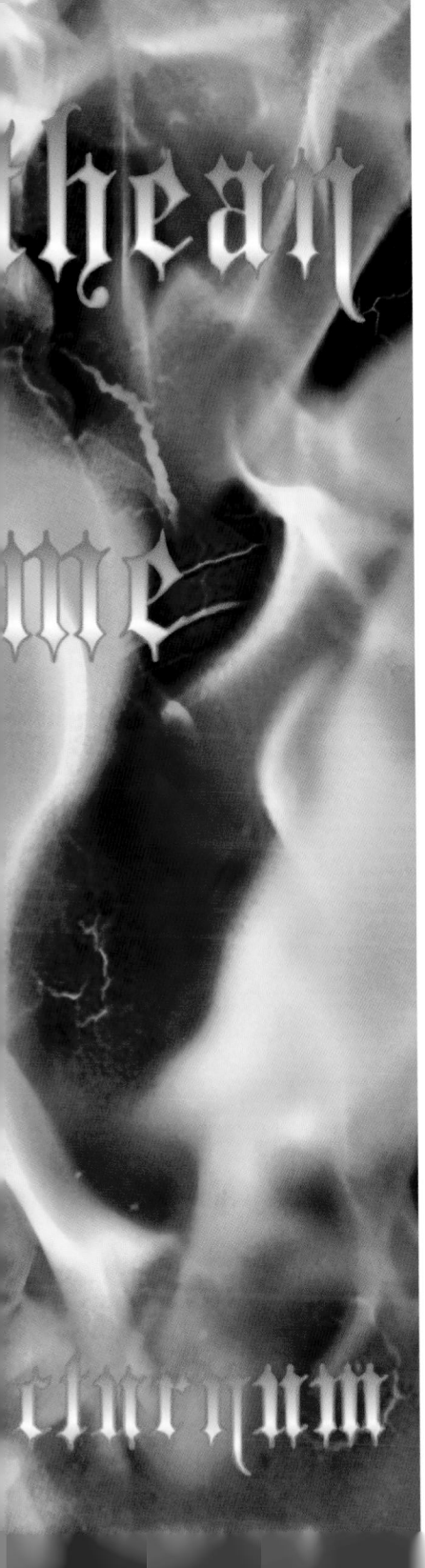

Jung's system was called analytical psychology and myths were a powerful tool, a psychological reality, and felt religion, myths, and occult symbols are parts of it all. For Jung, the Devil was more than a mere expression of individual repressions, and did not dismiss his symbolism as shallow selfishness and he insisted that there are two sides of reality. He called it pleroma, a yin yang stating Lucifer rebelling pushed God to develop deeper and higher wisdom. Without believing it was anything other than a mental construct, he nevertheless said evil must be faced, and named in order to face it within ourselves. Full confrontation of one's own dark nature, our secret needs, wants and desires.

Promethean Flame, 2007 Dark Moon Press. *Courtesy of Dark Moon Press.*

Jung, Tarot, and the Devil

Jung theorized that, when related to a psychological archetype, Tarot cards could be helpful in analysis, especially in symbolism contained within the Tarot could be extremely useful. By applying archetypes to the cards in the Tarot deck, Jung believed they could aid in finding solutions. For our example, in this archetype, the Rider-Waite card shows a winged, horned Devil, a black pedestal, and an inverted pentagram. The Devil is holding chains to a naked couple at his feet. Looking at it from a deeply symbolic level, we need to ask what exactly is holding us captive here. The chains are our own weaknesses and negative tendencies, and our inner fears. How do we rid ourselves of such feelings that hold us captive, and free ourselves from the Devil of our own making? The nudity is not about our sexuality and fear with sex, but the feeling of vulnerability and helplessness. In a sense this card helps us seek true knowledge, seeing past illusion.

Another writer who considers the archetypal significance of the Devil card in the Tarot deck is Sallie Nichols, author of *Jung and Tarot: An Archetypal Journey*. In keeping with the typical view of Satan, Nichols sees the Devil as a figure necessary to the evolution of humankind. "As long as our obedience to a moral code is automatic, we are not free." She says, "As long as we refuse to turn and confront our inner Devils – whatever form these may take – we are not human." In this vision, rather than a figure obsessed with the corruption of human beings, the Devil is a bringer of consciousness. "To be slavishly and unconsciously bound to even the most altruistic code," continues Nichols, "as surely marks one a creature of the Devil as to be victimized by one's own appetites." Jung decried was not madness. It was a sickness, not possession that the Devil was man dealing with fears, "animalistic mental activity."

THE DEVIL

The Devil Inside Us

With what is called a demonic archetype, we see again a similarity in thought to The Devil as a Tarot card image. That is to say when a person identifies with the demonic archetype, they are the type of person who loves debating, mind games, and enjoys riddles. Again, it does not totally operate from the standpoint of being evil despite the name, simply describes a certain way of thinking and personality that as such exhibits traits associated with classical stories of these beings. It could be said that the psychology of man is mirrored in Gods/the Devil dichotomy, in that the two opposite natures of "good and evil," exists in nearly equal measure. These metaphors, images, and symbols were experienced in the form of a sort of resonance in each of us, almost better to say it is a personality type. Usually considered negative or destructive are the psychopathic personalities that we identify as Sociopathic Styles (archetypical behaviors of a disturbed individual). In dealing further with the Devil as an archetype, deeply rooted in our psyche, Jung tells us of his personal meeting with the Red One, an imaginary figure in one of his fantasies. Jung wrote in *Liber Primus of the Red Book:*

> I KNOW JUST AS LITTLE WHO YOU ARE, AS YOU KNOW WHO I AM… SURELY THIS RED ONE WAS THE DEVIL, BUT MY DEVIL… I EARNESTLY CONFRONTED MY DEVIL AND BEHAVED WITH HIM AS WITH A REAL PERSON. THIS I HAVE LEARNED IN THE MYSTERIUM TO TAKE SERIOUSLY EVERY UNKNOWN WANDERER WHO PERSONALLY INHABITS THE INNER WORLD, SINCE THEY ARE REAL BECAUSE THEY ARE EFFECTUAL.

The Devil – God's Shadow

Freud's famous student, Psychologist Carl G. Jung, suggested that the darker aspects of human nature and the cosmos were merely alienated aspects of one's own personality, which he called the shadow, feeling that it gained form by those aspects of our lives which we try to repress. Yet in doing so, they manifest themselves in "rebellious" behavior or promiscuous behavior. Jung believed repression of destructive feelings creates the hidden negative parts of ourselves in all of us. The angel on one shoulder, while a demon whispers on the opposite side is the image that springs to my mind here. Most often, evil or the Devil itself is a personification of forbidden and repressed

desires that intrudes on us, apart from the tangible and physical world. The Devil has been thought of as a supernatural being that tempts, absolving us of guilt by the whole feeble "the Devil made me do it" excuse. By shifting the fault to an imagined incorporeal being, thus, then the boogeyman takes the responsibility off the guilty party's shoulders.

As for the notion of evil, according to Jung, is "terribly real for each and every individual if you can regard the principals of evil as a reality." (*Good and Evil in analytical psychology*, C.G. Jung). Christianity separates evil and understands it as something simplistic, an opposition to good, whereas Jung saw evil as that which needed to be recognized and in some ways embraced, in order for a person to be well balanced. With the original examples found in the Old Testament of Jehovah's kind nature as a benevolent God, peace and love as well as his "negative" aspects such as destructive floods and vengefulness "the wrath of God," the Christian deity is the sole bringer of death and destructive; his darker or Shadow nature was much clearer. Originally, the job of Satan as the angel was to accuse and punish the wicked *for* God. In the Book of Job, he enjoys his role as punisher and torturer of the wicked, and acts as man's adversary but *not* God's. All acts of punishment, vengeance, and temptation just so happened to be the darker, so called evil aspects are of God himself. The dark side of god himself seems to split away from himself and become mirrored in Satan, thus both God and the Devil could be viewed as one being, split into two divine aspects, "The Devil" then is God's Shadow if it is examined in a mythological/psychological analysis – in your basic stereotypical black/white or hero/villain role.

Jung writes a lot about Satan; in his own wording, it is very deep and complex as he details his personal vision of Christianity. He mixes theology and psychology in such a fashion it does make it difficult for the average person to grasp immediately. However, after going over it carefully, I take it to mean he is expressing that the idea that the godhead might embrace all opposites, including an area of what he terms "dark unconsciousness," and that in his psychoanalysis is that the Devil people visualize when hearing the name alone ironically contains other meanings subconsciously. Most people would be quite shocked to think of Lucifer as having any redeeming qualities, yet he does if you look at the nature of the classics in relation to a healthy mental state. This symbolism, the decent of Satan into the mortal realm, far from hindering humankind, actually brings him as The Light Bearer, as a friend to man, (again, like Prometheus, fire – light to see "truth" stolen from its keeper and giving it to man in each story was an unforgivable act, equal to the apple parable, where knowledge leads to questioning and advancement of man). The archetype of villain defies authority for man's benefit. Between the Old Testament and New Testament, the Devil's wickedness is formed while the goodness of God became emphasized. A human being will have a good and bad side, yet in time, will push aside their carnal and aggressive self, reducing it to the Shadow section of the mind. The Psychological viewpoint centers on Satan as being the primordial side of the human psyche which the majority of humanity seeks to control and eliminate, instead of accepting and making use of in a good way. As Freudian would call the id, Jung called the Shadow, which are the ideals of a "Satanic self" which the psychological view of modern religious Satanism actually desires to seek out and liberate in them – we'll look at this closely in the coming of the mid 1900s; an entire religion would be based primarily from the symbolic representation of Satan. (See Chapter Four.)

The Devil From Ancient Times

Where exactly, however, did the idea of an ultimate idea of an personification of The Devil begin, one must ask. Having poured over a hundred books to research this volume, I set out to find out the answer. Primitive man seems to indicate that religion evolved when man sought answers to his fears. In the most remote of worship, every culture long before Judeo-Christianity (indeed, any of the commonly understood Abrahamic religions) had a dark figure to place responsibility on or explain the tragedies of life. The unknowable causes fear as violent storms and nature catastrophes, animal attacks, diseases – especially in ancient times, was perceived as "evil" in primitive minds, usually attributed to angry gods long before science. Sacrifices were conducted to the gods by ancient pagans and Christians to appease their deities, long before witchcraft was accused of making human or animal sacrifices to the Devil. Early stages of religion developed by man lead us to the idea that fear is the cause of faith and religion overall in its infancy, and special awe was given to the powers of good and evil equally, says the author of *The History of the Devil and the Idea of Evil: From the Earliest Times to the Present Day,* Paul Carus.

Lucifer, Gustave Doré's 1866 illustration for *Paradise Lost* by John Milton.

Archangel Lucifer is a statue by Jacob Epstein in the Birmingham Museum and Art Gallery. *Photo courtesy Library of Congress*

Daniel Hopfer, Death and the Devil Surprising Two Women, circa 1500-10.

Personification of Evil

No one knows what culture first conceived the idea of a Devil, as there were so many cultures that existed simultaneously. However, it is a generally accepted idea that the Sumerian deities, Egyptian's Set and Persia's religion of Zoroaster who, as far as I can find, began the very first monotheistic religion around 505 B.C. and had the earliest "evil" deity.

Foremost, it is necessary to explain the most common concept of "evil" itself. As with so many broad labels and terms, it is difficult to define a simple ideal into one accepted definition, however, most religions and ethics authorities would allege evil refers to morally objectionable aspects of behavior and reason of human beings, committed by people void of conscience and who have a penchant for violence and wanton destruction without purpose. Evil, in a large sense, may be described as the sum of the opposition, to the desires and needs of individuals; among humans beings at least, the sufferings in which life exists. It is necessary to define the precise nature of the principle that imparts the character of evil to so great a magnitude of circumstances, and also to ascertain, as far as possible, to source from which it allegedly arises. The origin of evil is, like the origin of all things, inexplicable; it cannot be fitted into any theory of the design of the universe, simply because no such theory is possible. Physical evil includes all that causes harm to man, in which case it may be in the form of bodily injury, loss and tragedy, such as poverty, oppression, and disease. But these, say the skeptic, are instances of evil arising from imperfect social organization. Throughout history, as people search for meaning in existence, humanity has been faced with the problem of evil. The simple fact that humanity has caused itself immense suffering is a fact which cannot be ignored. But to look deeper for a root cause is another matter entirely, with both religion and philosophies attempting to develop explanatory systems that will emerge to cope with introspection of ourselves and society. We find ourselves looking into the mirror asking if it is merely we as a collective whole who create evil, or is it an outside force. Is it truly a necessary precondition of the universe, or merely an undesirable by-product of an imperfect cosmos we accidentally evolved out of? Is evil a subjective perception in a morally neutral universe, or could it be an absolute in itself, wholly independent of human existence at all. More directly to us as individuals, one asks: How should evil perpetrated by man be dealt with by society and by individuals. Religious people look to the existence of the beings that create, embody, or personify evil. Neither complex theories of philosophy nor mythological approaches/religions can simply explain away the sanity of an all-powerful, all-good creator in a world filled with suffering. The problem of evil and how Christianity explained it can be traced back to early man with Plato. He argued that evil was merely the privation of good, that it had no status of its own. While he, of course, acknowledged the existence of moral evils in the form of wars and mans deliberately selfish acts, he conveniently dismissed them or explained them away as a mere lack of peace or lack of truth. Early Christian theologians, such as Saint Augustine, were quick to accept this platform regarding evil, refusing from that point forward to recognize the incompatibility of the prevention of any original evil, against the power of the omnipotence of God. For if evil had no being, how could it exist as an incarnated in Lucifer; being pegged as an accident by the ultimate good would fly in the face of both reason and religious thought, thus an unanswered catch twenty-two!

As I worked my way through my Bachelors degree in Criminal Justice, I found that sociologists and crime behavioral professors by and large agreed with my thinking on the cause of our fellow man's desire to do harm to one another. People are not born evil as the early Church insists. We become that way by social conditioning and older influences in adults around us, and reinforced by our squalid living conditions, and apathy (the broken window theory.)

Of course, some young people in bad conditions push past obstacles and still become shining examples for others – I know, as I was in a severely troubled childhood, yet decades later believe I have risen above it all. It is through fear of the unknown and fear of punishment, people in charge get others to bend to their will. It is due to consequences that man does not do foul to one another, not out of compassion, else we would not have need for a judicial system nor prisons, if all that prevented people from crime was conscience. Say, for example: If you could get away with a bank heist or do away with an enemy who scarred you or a loved one, would you not do them harm? Would you not commit either crime if no one would ever catch you? It is fear that governs us or the common sense, "If I get caught, I'll be in jail." Sociopaths even avoid crime for it would prevent them from doing what they wish to do, not out of being pure of heart.

Yet, we find that even among the most pure of beliefs in the world, evil does exist. Maiming an animal or another human is wrong you insist? Yet it continues to happen. In fact, biblically speaking, God gave the creatures unto Adam for his use. What has been done with this "use"? Senseless destruction and harm to the undeserving is evil, so the act of wiping out thousands of accused heretics at the stake by religious zealots, while clear cutting millions of acres of plant and animal life to the brink of extinction, all due to early Christian explorers and their descendants with the attitude of "right of emanate domain"– does this not fall under the category of evil? We all feel evil in our hearts but most shove it away and deny its existence in ourselves.

Humanity as a whole cannot fathom that they, by choice, are fully responsible for such things, so in order to cope with the vileness of particular behaviors place the blame upon a larger force. My speculation is that collective minds seem to need to label a particular origin in order to accept it. Without tangible proof of its existence, the ideal cause is then given a name, i.e., The Devil, Old Scratch, Lucifer, etc., and the collective accepts this figure to be real over the ages by social conditioning outside of religious circles. In the 1970s, people polled in the United States believed in the Devil and it shows no sign of diminishing even though America has increasingly become secular in nature. Let us look at the evolution of our collective perception of him.

Satan's Pagan DNA

We typically associate evil as not having good qualities, and anything associated with it (the Shadow or The Devil) as bad. In myths, we can examine many stories before Christianity where evil is balanced with good, in different forms. Cultures assimilated by Judeo-Christianity took traits of their dark gods, and when force did not work, sought to sway the conquered nations to convert by twisting preexisting myths into their own, blurring each faith together to pull new followers in from the old religion; for example, The Native American Church uses sage instead of incense like the Catholics do.

With certain faiths, good and evil was a needed balance and in some cases they were manifestations shown as brothers. With Hindu and Egypt especially, we have Shiva and Kali originally manifested as benevolent, but nature's order of creation and destruction were picked apart, and disregarding the creative aspects, the rest thoroughly became demonized. Attributes of Set, Hades, and Pan became twisted physical characteristics of Satan. Death from Hades, Hel, and Egypt's land of the dead influenced Hell. The red of Hell due to the tint of hellfire, scorched sand with blood in war became associated with the Devil's appearance, and from Egypt's god, Set and his followers who had red hair. In Revelations, red is associated with the red dragon, Lucifer. Black came from a variety of sources, from the fear of darkness (a void of color, the "goodness" of light) where we become afraid of what may happen to us. From primitive man needing fire to stay both warm and keep away the unknown, we subconsciously attribute black with evil. This is why figures like witches to modern-day arch-villains like Darth Vader wore black, whereas angels and the good cowboys in old films are always depicted in white. Here we fully understand color association with the nature of people and higher beings. This goes back as far as the goddesses like Shiva being black, as is Kali. The Chaos in darkness from a Biblical view, along with the release of forces in magic containing energy is presented in rituals, orgies, and wild fests.

During the Middle Ages, we see the look of the archetype change drastically, from a heavenly angel more beautiful than all the rest to suddenly become a monster. All of this and the obvious aspects of the Devils personality changes can be broken down into its multitude of origins. Let's look at them closely.

Horns came to play one of the most prominent characteristics of Satan's look. The idea of horned images being manifestations of just a single god was an attempt of Christians to suppress worship of them and associate them with their forming idea of the Devil. We'll explore this in more depth in the chapter on sex and the Devil, but suffice to say for the time being, it was a borrowed element from the old god Pan. The trident wielding monster was the invention of over-active imaginations in the nineteenth century, a response by Christian moralists protesting the advent of Greek and Roman mythology in artworks done by popular painters during that time. The story of "Percy Jackson and the Lightning Thief" shows Poseidon's son wielding his trident for a modern depiction example. Look around the internet or if you are lucky enough, travel to the Louvre and see the art of the Renaissance and before. Prior to this time, a man in black or an animal, being a dog or goat mostly, with the human figure with bat wings and sometimes talons of a bird was how Satan was portrayed. As far back as the Paleolithic era, which extends from 2.5 million years ago to 10,000 BC, in the Caverne des Trois Freres at Ariege, France shows a carving on a cave wall of a horned figure walking

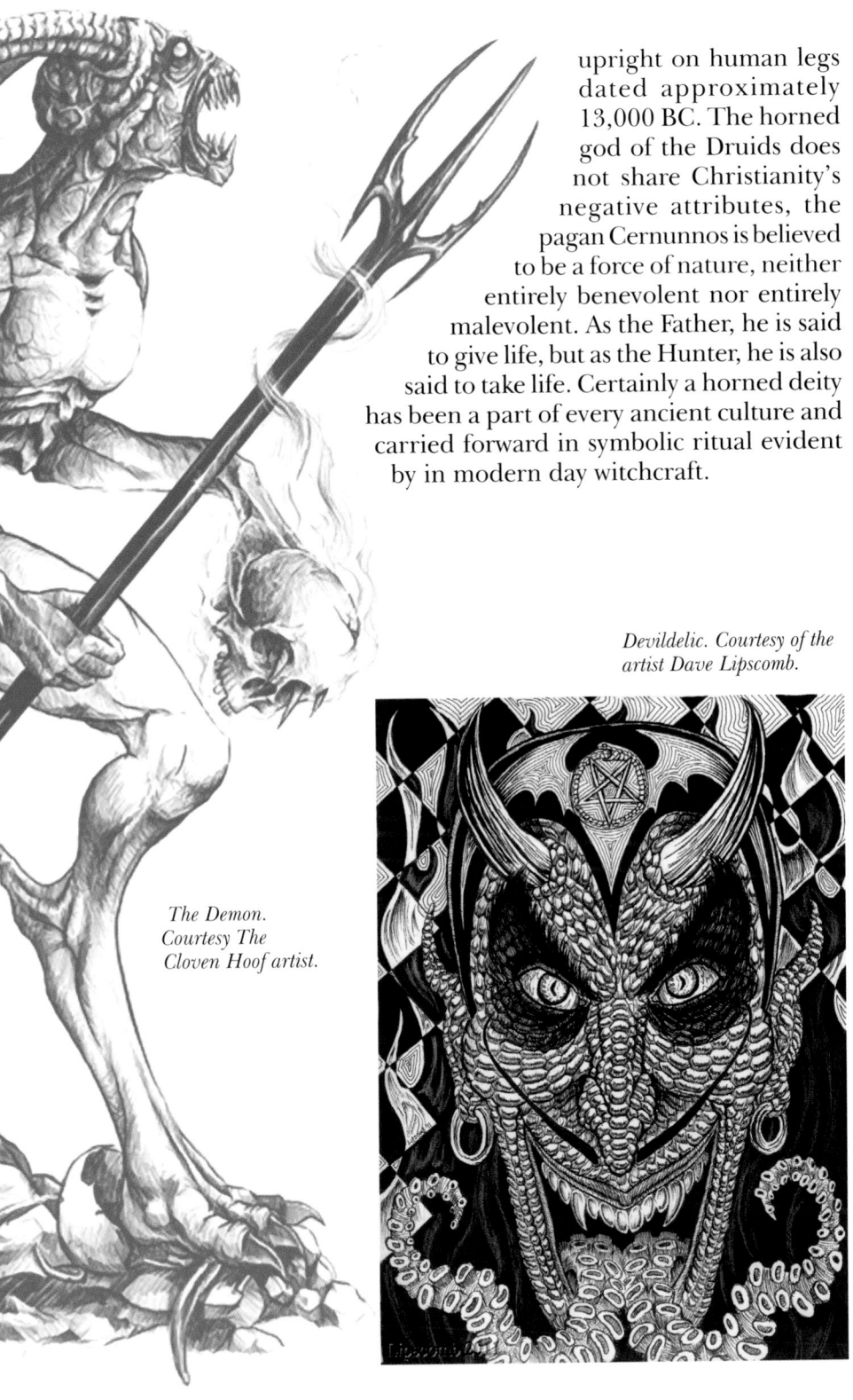

upright on human legs dated approximately 13,000 BC. The horned god of the Druids does not share Christianity's negative attributes, the pagan Cernunnos is believed to be a force of nature, neither entirely benevolent nor entirely malevolent. As the Father, he is said to give life, but as the Hunter, he is also said to take life. Certainly a horned deity has been a part of every ancient culture and carried forward in symbolic ritual evident by in modern day witchcraft.

Devildelic. Courtesy of the artist Dave Lipscomb.

The Demon. Courtesy The Cloven Hoof artist.

In researching further, I discovered Pan is the root word for "panic," the wild debauchery in the orgies, a force harnessed by the Greeks and occultists. We learned of Baphomet aspects and his connection to the occult in *Promethean Flame*. Hostility of the animal (and Freud might say the penetration aspect was sexual in nature) contributed to the trident of Poseidon, later given to the Devil. Horns were used for drinking, the powder of animal horns in many cultures like Asian use for sexual stamina in apothecary still are sold today. Horns on the Devil equate power of war and lust, the common hand salute among metal heads at concerts has been a given for years. Cernunnos and the satyrs and Greek god Pan all had horns long before Lucifer evolved into a horny old Devil! The cloven hooves of goats, believed to be possessed by unclean animals, and hairy legs of Pan became traits of the medieval Satan. Who hasn't seen the 1986 movie *Legend* and been delighted by Tim Curry as the

Devil? Pan's father, Hermes, was very much a phallic deity, and no doubt the wings on Hermes' legs attributed to the wings on the Devil as much as the angel wings from the fallen angel Lucifer did. The Devil was thought to be the prince of the Earth and ruled the sky. Wealth associated with Satan was more than greed being sinful; it came from him lording over the Earth and its treasures. In various aspects of the underworld, Hades especially, hoarded wealth reflecting the riches the world holds, like gems, gold, and silver. Hecate was the sister of Artemis, a dark goddess of night and the underworld. Practitioners of occultism utilizing a feminine side most often use Hecate, Kali, and Artemis as their feminine side of the god/goddess balance. There are some others as we'll explore in the next chapter. Prometheus is important in the formation of the Devil in his personality, influencing Milton, which I'll cover later, in the archetypical role of the antihero, who loved man more than the wishes of his higher god.

Enlightenment in the Garden of Eden by author.

The pagan influences of the
Devil, art by author 2009.

Devil in Hell, candle photo.
Courtesy of author.

Lilith. Courtesy Jason Sorrel 2007.

JASON SORRELL-2007

Egypt's Influence on The Devil

Set, although not directly a Devil per se, is one of the oldest-known aspects that existed as performing the duties of antagonist to a Sungod of light and ruled over Hell. Set was also called Typhon by the Greeks (iron was called the bones of Typhon); he was called the ruler of the south, is the slayer and deity of the desert. Considered an enemy of life, he rules the moon, night, and the afterlife. The Lord of the Desert was worshipped by guide travelers across the dessert. When the deceased travel to Set, he received offerings in tombs. As the worship of his opponent Osiris grew, he slowly became a Satan of sorts, the opponent of the "good" god. Setians, who worshipped Set and dyed their hair red to match the red of the dessert, were some of the earliest "Devil worshippers" of all time. Interestingly, similar to the fall of the angel Lucifer, falling from Heaven was a story I found of a serpent carrying a Pharaoh to Earth with lightning, as was much like the classic lightning bolt of Satan striking the Earth to find Hell in the center of the earth.

The Sumerian Devil

Around the year 3000 BC, before the Babylonian and Israelite nations in the Mesopotamia were a powerful nation known as Accad, the Accadians were a dark-skinned people – given the area they inhabited (Babylon tablets referred to them as red skinned) and they gave rise to the ancient Semites. The Assyrians spoke of a serpent of the deep, known as Tiamtu, Some speculate this is where the serpent in the garden of Eden came from, but it is not a fact. The serpent was conquered by the Sungod, Bel-Merodach, who goes on to fight the next incarnation of the evil demon as it shows itself as seven wicked storm demons. The god of the Assyrians is three fold, called Anu, Ea, and Bel. Thought to be male and female with the divine father as Anu, the mother Ea and Bel, the Christ offspring god form. Marduk (or Merodach) fought Tiamat the evil one, was horned, clawed with tail, had wings, and scales that were frightening to ancient man. Artists often portrayed them on items to scare the demons with their own hideous appearance. In the Louvre museum, an image of a demon with a dog's head, eagle feet, lion's paws, and a scorpion tail has an inscription that identifies it is a spirit of the south wind, a hot and scorching desert of Arabia. This could very well be where the fire of Hell and the abode of these creatures came from. Creatures called the Nirgalli are very similarly described, but more human with lion heads and eagle feet, as art in the British Museum shows. Some aspects of the Underworld, demons and a trinity of God and the Devil with minions predated the Hebrews' Satan and his demons stemming from pre-Babylonian civilization of the Assyrians. The ancient Egyptian and Babylonians clearly helped create the Old Testament. Religious leaders after the Assyrians stamped out the faiths of their ancestors, taking from it what they wanted and demonizing what they did not want.

Monotheism and Duality of Good and Evil

With the rise of ancient Persia, the first major religion focusing on the duality of a pure good God and an evil as a single source came from Zoroaster, around the sixth century, doctrines five centuries before Christ. Arhiman became the archfiend, a snake-like deity of their enemy the Scythians, believing this Devil to be an independently existing entity representing contradictory principals. Zoroaster attributed good and evil respectively to two mutually hostile principles called Ormuzd and Arhriman. Each was independent of the other; but eventually, the good were to be victorious with Ormuzd, and Arhriman and his evil followers were to be expelled from the world. The dualistic doctrine of the Persians explained that Ahura Mazda created the Earth, Heavens, and mortal Man, that good men were to pray to in thanks. The personification of evil, Arhiman, rules evil men when they die in Hell, and the Savior will one day resurrect the dead and bring both the dead and the pure living to him as immortals to Heaven, similar to the Christians doctrine of Revelations centuries later. This mythological dualism passed to the sect of the Manichees, whose founder, Manes, held that matter was essentially evil, and therefore could not be in direct contact with God, deriving the notion from the Gnostic sects, as the evil of matter. They held a confusing theory that the world was to have been formed by a merger between God and impure matter. Evil was thought to be a result from the misuse of created free will.

Arhiman himself is shown in art with the Persian King slaying a deformed unicorn that has eagle and lion traits (much taken from the Assyrians art) in both sculptures. A sect of Izedis, the first Devil worshippers, were discovered in Mesopotamia.

Early Christianity and The Devil

The ancient Israelites sacrificed a goat to the demon of the dessert, Azazel, mentioned in the Bible in Leviticus, "one (goat) for the Lord, and the other for Azazel..." This is where scapegoat came from as well, as Yahaveh's goat is a sin offering and the other is cast out into the dessert or hurled from a cliff to die shattered at the bottom, in order to carry the curses and sins with it. Both the power of good and evil are at this time considered equal. Symbolically this practice continues but in a subtler fashion. We apply the term "scapegoat" to individuals and groups who are accused of causing misfortune. Thus, they seem to relieve others, of their own responsibilities, and to strengthen their sense of power or righteousness. Few remember that originally the scapegoat was a human or animal victim chosen for sacrifice to the underworld god to heal the community.

The Laws of Exodus provided for capital punishment for witchcraft, and in Leviticus, "A man also or a woman that hath a familiar spirit, or that is a wizard, shall surely be put to death; they shall stone them with stones: their blood shall be upon them." (Lev. Xx 27) Interestingly, however, it is always that the work of wizards, witches, healers like midwives (called witches by the Inquisition) and Shamanic healers of all types were condemned to death deserved death while saints and prophets works were acts for God when the same results were had. Only when death occurred it was God's will, all other times it was the Devil's hand. Similar deeds yet vastly different outcomes, depending on what the healers' faith was. One performed miracles; the other ironically was a servant of the Devil.

From Angel to Demon

In analyzing the concept of the Devil from its strongest precedents in our world is from a Biblical perspective, keeping with the various times and places in which it evolved. From the Fall of Lucifer to the serpent in the Garden of Eden on to Revelations, we discover evolution of the archetype there as well. Satan started out as an angel in Heaven's court, the most beautiful of them all. As Christianity grew, the Devil became the embodiment of evil. Widely accepted thought in modern and very late Medieval times was that the fallen angels were associated with Satan, the enemy of God. This contributed to art and literature for centuries, spawning classic depictions by Dore and Raphael to written works by Milton's *Paradise Lost* and Dante's *The Divine Comedy*, men who I discussed in great detail in previous works. Archangels and fallen angels exist in numerous religious traditions beyond Christianity, each with legends very similar to Catholicism. Faiths such as Judaism, Islam, and Zoroastrianism include parallel ideas of the casting out of Lucifer and a full third of the Heavenly host.

The name "Lucifer" is Latin, meaning "light-bearer" and is a Roman astrological term for Morning Star, also known as the planet Venus. The Bible (see Isaiah 14:3-20) speaks of someone who is given the name of Day Star or Morning Star as fallen from heaven. The same Latin word is used of the Morning Star in Peter 1:19 and elsewhere with no relation to Satan. In Latin, the word Lucifer, meaning Light-Bringer from lux, lucis, light, and ferre, to bear, bring, is a name for the Morning Star. This passage was later applied to the prince of the demons, and so the name Lucifer came to be used for Satan. I find it interesting that the Bible never clearly designates Lucifer as the Morning Star or as the Day Star; however, it does clearly designate Christ as the Morning Star. Originally, Lucifer as a name was nothing more than a Roman deity, the male counterpart to the female Venus, Greek correspondent Aphrodite, who was the Goddess of Love and Beauty, Lucifer was the God of the Morning Star. The concepts in Milton and Dante's works shaped the idea that Lucifer was a poetic anti-hero, encouraging free will and pride, the strongest traits in the angel Lucifer that lead to his expulsion in the first place. The consequences of free will include responsibility for our very human emotions.

Lucifer's rebellion was considered the greatest of the seven sins. Being the first angel created, he was second in beauty, intelligence, and powerful only to God. Becoming ambitious, he raised his throne up to his creators' height, an act that was mirrored in other religions such as the Caanite's deities. In the Muslims' Qur'an, God had asked the angels to bow before God's creation as it was made in his image. Lucifer refused and demanded that man worship him, as he was made first. The Fall of Man and the Fall of Lucifer were parallels, as it is said the root of all sin, in both man and angels, is the twin sin of unbelief and pride—the refusal to submit to God's will. This was the original sin of Satan, rejecting God's Word and trying to become God himself – "I will ascend into heaven, I will exalt my throne above the stars of God: ... I will be like the most High..." (Isaiah 14:13,14). Seeing as Christ was made from man's image, the scorn of Lucifer doubled, and motivated the temptations of Christ on Earth.

The Devil of the Middle Ages

Around the early 1450s, during what was known as the Byzantium era of the Medieval period, the church placed more emphasis on the monasticism and mysticism than did the Eastern Orthodox. The two different sects of the Eastern and Western churches are lengthy, but suffice to say, the Eastern section paid less attention to the Devil; so we will focus more on the era of Europe that most tend to think of when recalling the time shortly after the Crusades and the fall of Constantinople.

Believing the Devil and his demons to be once good angels whose pride made them fall from grace, these scholars felt the primary purpose of Satan was to tempt man away from God as well. Believing at this time that Satan was both God's enemy and servant to tempt, man is still able to exert free will, and capable in the future of salvation by God should both choose. Others disagreed, and from the tenth to the fourteenth centuries, the debate on both redemption and places of rank among the fallen were argued. During this period, diablogy, or the study of demons, was split into two schools of thought.

In reading Jeffery Burton Russell's deep examination into the histories of the Devil, I found that according to one theory, the Devil was subordinate to God, yet wielded great powers on Earth. They felt God had two sons, Satanael the elder son, Christ the younger. Satanael grew dissatisfied serving and rebelled, taking a third of the heavenly host of angels with him. Mimicking God's creation, he swore to create his own version. He then created Adam and breathed life into it, only to find the life seeped out in the form of a snake from Adam's foot. Failing, Satanael asked the Lord for help in his work, and in return, he offered co-governship over the human race. After doing so, they together, created Eve, at which time Satanael turned himself into the snake and deceived the first human couple into

A woman torn in pieces by the Devil woodcut art 1500.
Photo courtesy Library of Congress.

Temptation of St. Anthony by artist Lucas Cranach.

betraying God's will. God in turn punished Satanael by changing his once-beautiful form into ugliness and took away his power to create. Further, this sect believed Christ never died, so the cross is a lie and miracles were the work of demons. And that, in the end, Christ/Michael will destroy Satanael.

The priesthood thought that magic was natural, not supernatural, and would combine magic and prayer, invocations, and supplications for the good of their congregation. My thought is that all the other is, in reality, the same thing, simply a different word for the same act, regardless of Pagan or Christian. The intent is fully the same, regardless of the faith that made use of it. Other schools of thought disagreed, coming from the practical ideas of Aristotle who had little or no room for magic and occultism, and all workings were demonic in nature. For Aristotle and other pragmatic thinkers, "evil" is a necessary aspect of the constant changes of matter, and has in itself no real existence.

The Stoics conceived evil in a somewhat similar manner, as due to necessity; the power of God harmonizes the evil and good in a changing world, and moral evil proceeds from the folly of mankind, not from the Divine will.

As Christians beliefs system shaped and developed further, the role Satan grew along with it. Unfortunately, this was accompanied by the dark age fears that caused power-hungry and fearful people to label those who did not agree with them to be in league with Satan, combined with blind superstition and fear of the Devil lurking around every corner. This widespread paranoia grew and made it quite simple to make the claim that someone was an enemy of the Church, which led to the persecution of anyone not in agreement with the early Church.

In the area of Central and Eastern Europe, comprising Germany, Austria, Hungary, and the Czech Republic, the Devil was never fully absorbed into the Christian mythos as Satan, but remained as he had always been, a slender, horned, bearded, fur-covered half-man of the woods. Under the regional names Krampus, Schwarze Peter (Black Peter), joined Saint Nicholas on his rounds of gift-giving, originally on December 6th, but eventually on Christmas Day, December 25th. In the early part of the twentieth century, it was the custom during December to send humourous Krampus postcards to friends. The example shown here, dated 1932, contains a bit of verse in German: Gruss von Krampus! Wenn im Herzen brennt das Feuer freut sich das schwarze Ungeheuer. The English translation: Greetings from Krampus! When the fire burns in the heart the black monster rejoices. The dancing Krampus', job was to punish children who had behaved badly during the year. Unlike the conventional Christian Devil, Krampus is usually depicted with only one cloven hoof, not two.

Temptations of St. Anthony.

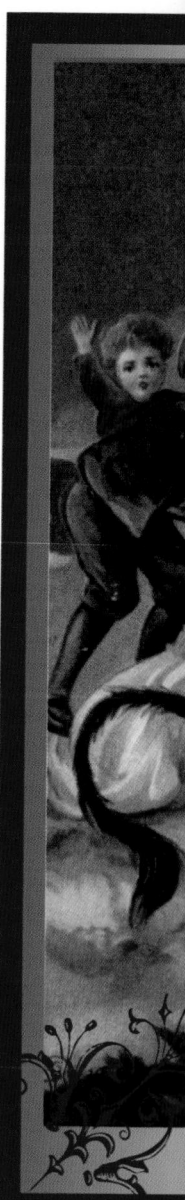

Close up of St. Michael vanquishing
Satan by Renaissance painter Raphael.

Illuminated manuscript, Middle Ages date and artist unknown. *Courtesy* The Ninth Gate Magazine *published by the author.*

he Krampus

Krampus card, artist unknown. *Photo courtesy Library of Congress.*

The Muslims' Devil

In or around the year 610, Muhammad grew up exposed to Jewish, Christian, and Pagan ideology. He claimed to have been visited by Gabriel and instructed to write the Qur'an. In 622, Muhammad traveled the Mediterranean area and the Middle East, and Islam grew. It is unclear if Satan in this version was a higher rank or not when he fell. It is important to note that in the three Abrahamic religions of Christianity, Judaism, and Islam, that an all powerful God exists, and a Devil. In the Islamic faith, Iblis is the primary name in the Qur'an, the holy book of the Middle East. Known as Satan, or "al-Shaitan" (meaning "born in anger") is the general term used to refer to all of the evil spirits in alliance with Iblis, but which is often simply Iblis. Iblis is ruler of the spirits of the Jinn, creatures made of smokeless fire by God Jinn, creature of smoke and fire. A jinni is where we get Genie from, told and made famous by the "Ali Baba and the Forty Thieves" fable. Like the Christian tale, al-Shaitin disobeyed Allah (the Islamic God) out of envy. He tempted Adam and Eve with forbidden fruit and thus was sent to Jahannam, or Hell. Like Christianity later, this form of the Devil struck a bargain with God to test both Jinn and man while roaming the Earth while tempting and misguiding them. He was condemned consequently by Allah to Jahannam Islam's Hell. He tempts humans through the whisper of sinful ideas in their head and false suggestion. In the end, it is believed, he will be cast into with others who disobeyed Allah's true message to mankind, while those who successfully try to follow a righteous path will be rewarded with the pleasures of Jannah or Paradise. The Devil' purpose here is to discourage humans from obeying God. The Qur'an does not specifically make their Devil an enemy of Allah; they are simply viewed as creations, with the single enemy of Allah being humanity itself. In Islamic faith, everything is God's will, including suffering and evil, for a purpose. The soul of man the Qur'an claims is prone to evil. The biggest difference is that all deeds, good and bad, stem from Allah himself. Christianity and Islam share the idea that personal evil in life is experienced because of the Devil. As with Christianity, indeed with all monotheism, Islamic faith provides no clear answer as to why an all powerful good allows evil to exist.

The Muslims were condemned despite the similarities of the two faiths. Muhammad was thought to be the Devil incarnate and his followers the servants of Satan, writes the author of *The Devil: A Biography*, (Henry Holt & Co., 1996), and this hysteria continued in the name of saving people from Satan for decades to come. One only need look at the madness of the Inquisition and the eventual destruction of many indigenous civilizations in the name of religion to bear witness to the reality of what happens when fear becomes more powerful than the good intentions an idea may have begun with.

During the Feast day is that of Jam; the various Yezidi groups converge at a place called Lalishand, where they present to the worshippers, the Peacock icon, representing Malek Taus, during a seven day celebration. This coincides with the ancient Zoroastrian feast day, one of many coincidences that lead some scholars to make a connection between the two religions.

The Yezidi beliefs are a complicated mixture of Islam with Gnostic, Jewish, and Shamanistic elements; and worship centers around Angels – Yezidi is from the Arabic word for angel and Melek Taus, or Peacock Angel, was Lucifer. To the Yezidism, Lucifer is the creator of the material world, and is not a fallen angel, nor the enemy of God. Instead, they claim that Lucifer was forgiven for his transgressions, and those who revere him are the spiritual elect of humanity – Satan is portrayed as a wise teacher rather than a tempter. The Yezidi have long been accused of Devil worship because of the misunderstandings of their religion.

The Traditional Qur'an (sura 114) provides a supplication for mankind, aimed at fighting the tempting of ash-Shay tan and his minions:

> Say: I seek refuge with the Lord and Cherisher of Mankind,
> The King (or Ruler) of Mankind,
> The god (or judge) of Mankind,
> From the mischief of the Whisperer (of Evil), who withdraws (after his whisper),
> (The same) who whispers into the hearts of Mankind,
> Among Jinns and among men.

Luciferians and the Charthers

For centuries, Catholic scholars would debate the subtleties of the Devil's origin, his fall, and place in our world, without ever facing the basic contradiction of divine benevolence with the presence of evil. The solution had, in fact, been provided in the first two centuries after Christ, but was declared heretical and suppressed by the Church. This was accomplished within the system of Christian Gnosticism.

The Gnostics dispensed with the infamous contradictions in mainstream Christian theology by dropping the assumption that the Ultimate God must also be the Ultimate Good. In a sense, the Gnostics returned to polytheistic while holding onto certain aspects of Christian doctrine, such Jesus as man's Savior and not connected with evil at all. One of the main teachings of Gnostic ideals was that the individual soul must attain gnosis – that is, self-knowledge, and to transcend the evil materialistic world becoming one with the Jesus. Obviously, they were greatly influenced by Buddhist missionaries to the Nile; Gnosticism was ruthlessly condemned nearly wiped out by the Catholic Church, but survived by way of mystic Christian groups such as the Cabbala, Rosicrucian's, and other secret societies. The Gnostics were obsessed with the problem of evil, claiming the Lord Christ and the Devil happened to be God's manifestations of his paradoxical unity. He was an object of veneration, for he was feared, but the Gnostic's worship was directed toward the Christ, who offered deliverance from the evils of the world. Ironically, the ability of the Gnostic fathers to consciously address the inherent contradictions of contemporary theologies is what caused them to be persecuted and burned as heretics.

The time of the Charthers, in 1150, marked a new stage for Lucifer, radically influencing the part the Devil and his minions were to play in the world. As Gnostic believed the world was evil and incapable of being redeemed, they had certain sympathy for the Devil akin to the Romantic Period creatives who saw Lucifer as an anti-hero to be both pitied and admired. (We'll look at this in Chapter Three.) The Charthers saw Lucifer as a martyr bound for eternity by an overbearing, all powerful tyrant, and that Lucifer was the maker of and ruler of the Earth. Earlier sects believed the Old Testament Yahweh was, in fact, the Devil, based on the beliefs of earlier Gnostics. Through studying ancient texts, the founders of Gnostics believed that an older Semitic deity of chaos and evil that was worshipped in the same area was the same as the God of the Old Testament. In the Gnostic Charthers thinking, the Devil played a vital job necessary to the cosmos by saving God's goodness and holding Yahweh to task for good and evil in the world. The Church despised the Charthers for many reasons, one of which was that they allowed women to have the role of reverend.

In 1215, the Catholic Church council addressed the threat of the Charthers, and considered them heretics very similarly as they did the with the Knights Templar. The Catholic Church considered these sects Luciferian, or inverse Christians, what is today in the modern media called Satanist/ Devil worship. I will go into more detail in future chapters describing the differences in the two as well as the commonalities. According to stories I discovered (and made more famous by *The Da Vinci Code*), Mary Magdalene was the Grail of legend. In Otto Rhan's book *Lucifer's Court: A Heretic's Journey in Search of the Light Bringers*, I read how the scholar goes into great detail of the Charthers and the 200 pacifist's fiery deaths by the hands of the Church in the year 1244 at the foothills of the Pyrenees's mountains. The wrath of the Church once again obliterated any major school of thought contrary to their teachings. Reputedly, the Charthers held Black Masses in the mountain cathedrals, sometimes involved the perversion and defilement of Catholic religious practices, and later, still made infamous by a few individuals exposed in scandal by having celebrated in the French court of Louis XIV. The infamous Mass involved the sacrifice of infants or maidens, and a general orgy among the participants during which ties of marriage and family were completely disregarded. The best accounts of this sort of ultimate depravity are to be read in the Marquis de Sade's novel *Justine*. This Mass was done in England by members of the Hell-Fire Club, which was an inspiration to the founding of the Church of Satan. As with the Templars, heresies attributed to the Charthers were sexual orgies, homosexual unions, scarifies to the Devil, infanticide, and cannibalism. Spreading this hysteria was a propaganda machine that the Charthers were servants of the Devil. It was around this time that the Jews were blamed most strongly for the death of Christ, Muslims were constantly considered evil since the Crusades, and much of the religious right we feel today stemmed from this era that is witnessed in Europe that was stirred during anti-Semitism of World War II. Fanatic Reverend Montague Summers wrote of the Charthers: "They openly worshipped Satan, repudiating Holy Mass and the Passion, rejecting Holy Baptism for some foul ceremony of their own." Of course, even decades after everyone else condemned the atrocities of the Great Inquisition, Montague Summers applauded their efforts, so his opinion holds little merit.

Lucifer's status as a Saint is a matter of controversy. In 1874, John Henry Blunt wrote *Dictionary of Sects, Heresies, Ecclesiastical Parties, and Schools of Religious Thought*, and in it he said,

> THE CHURCH OF CAGLIARI CELEBRATED THE FEAST OF A SAINT LUCIFER ON THE 20TH OF MAY. TWO ARCHBISHOPS OF SARDINIA WROTE FOR AND AGAINST THE SANCTITY OF LUCIFER. THE CONGREGATION OF THE INQUISITION IMPOSED SILENCE ON BOTH PARTIES, AND DECREED THAT THE VENERATION OF LUCIFER SHOULD STAND AS IT WAS. THE BOLLANDISTS DEFEND THIS DECREE OF THE CONGREGATION, CONTENDING THAT THE LUCIFER IN QUESTION IS NOT THE AUTHOR OF THE SCHISM, BUT ANOTHER LUCIFER WHO SUFFERED MARTYRDOM IN THE PERSECUTION OF THE VANDALS.

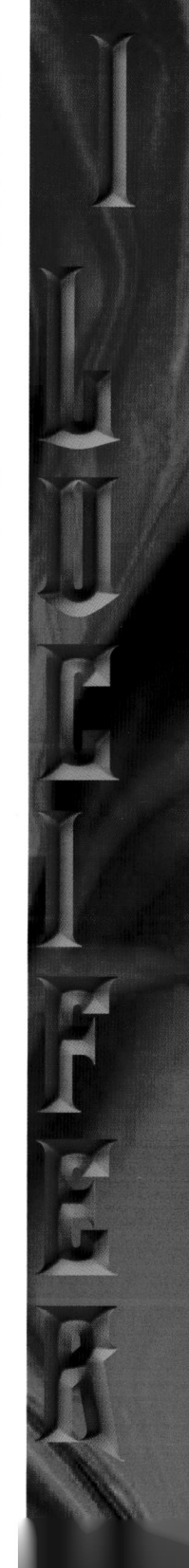

The Age of the Reformation and the Devil

By the time of the Reformation, late 1400s and early 1500s, there was a slight shift in how the Devil was perceived. Now interpreting him in psychological terms and less as a physical being, he became more separated from man. He then became a thought of fortune, power, and other worldly pleasures. At this time, Christianity was divided by conservatives of Rome and progressive Protestants who opposed the traditions. The anti reformation was held by Jesuits who frowned on freedom, scientific discovery, and pursuit of the truth. It comes to no shock to me that the inquisition was shaped by such rigid thinking. Luther saw the Devil in everything and even went so far as to call the pope an incarnation of Satan and the Roman Church as the kingdom of the Devil. To Luther, the Devil was real and a servant of the Lord in his own way. He claimed to see the evil one while translating the Bible and hurled his inkwell at him.

Various fiction involving the Devil came about around this time, which we shall deeply explore in how art and literature shaped our collective concept of Lucifer in a later chapter when milestone works like Milton changed the Devil into a sympathetic character in *Paradise Lost*, perhaps one of the modern world's most epic religious fiction.

In Venice, in 1550, the existence of the Devil, Hell, and the virgin birth was broached by the unorthodox Italian Anabaptist, but few until the Enlightenment period would pay any attention. After the Inquisition and hundreds of thousands of innocent pagan, Christian, and atheists died for nothing, the Devil seemed less villainous, and the witch craze had died down to almost nothing in all of Europe. In 1563, Johann Weir was a skeptic that wrote a criticism of demonology and witchcraft in *On Magic* as did, by 1693, *The Enchanted World* by Balthazaar Bekker, declared the belief in Devils, witches, and trials against them – as well as "the existence of the Devil was superfluous assumption. He wrote at the end of the sixteenth century that a personalized, individualistic Devil was a hoax" as he attacked the fervor of the witch hunts, coming to the conclusion that it was all fraud and therefore after argued that Satanists could not be prosecuted on the grounds that human beings can have no pact with that which does not exist. The common man during this time began to see religion as subjective and in having less faith in possessions and exorcisms, but yielded more in the way of introspection of themselves. The idea of the Devil did not alter much in the eyes of the Church or religion as a whole after this point; however, in culture among people all over, we will see his relevance change in during the Age of Enlightenment in Chapter Three on.

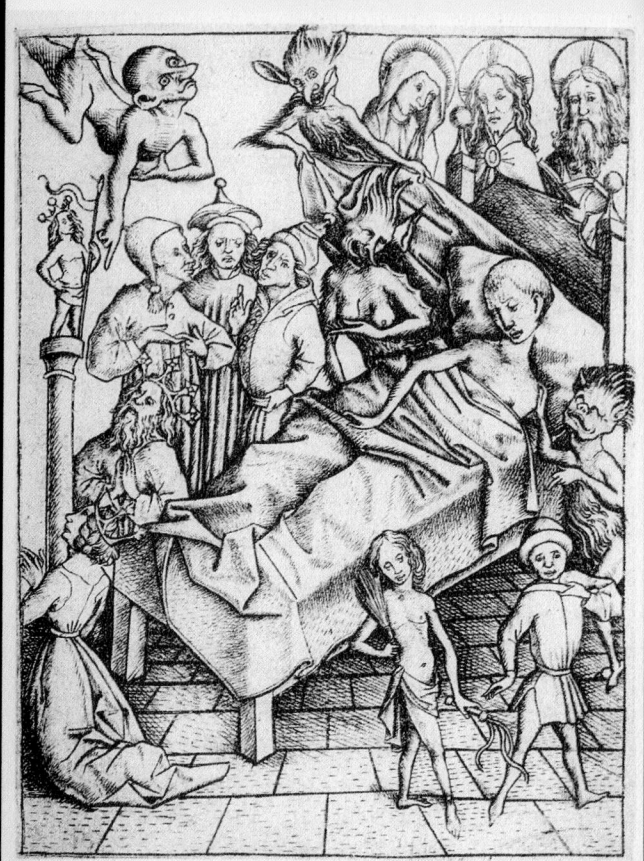

Chapter Two

Hell: Fact or Fiction?

Meister E., Le-tentazioni, Andreas Vesalius.

> *"Better to reign in Hell than serve in Heaven."*
>
> ~ Satan, John Milton's *Paradise Lost*

Many religious traditions believe in a place of suffering and punishment in the afterlife. Religions usually fall within two types of this suffering with a linear span that often depicts Hell as endless, whereas those with a cyclic version often depict Hell as an intermediate place of languishing between incarnations of rebirth. As Lauren Paine, author of *The Hierarchy of Hell* says,

Last Judgement, depicted by Fra Angeleco in the 1400s.

LATER CONCEPTS OF HELL ENLARGED UPON THE TORMENT, THE DARKNESS, THE DIRE PUNISHMENT, BUT NOT SO MUCH THAT THE EARLIER EGYPTIAN AND MUCH EARLIER PREHISTORIC IDEAS WERE NOT SO RECOGNIZABLE. IN THEORY, HELL EVOLVED RIGHT ALONG WITH MAN. IT CHANGED AS THE ERAS AND EPOCHS OF MAN CHANGED, IN EXACTLY THE SAME WAY THAT MAN'S GODS OR GOD CHANGED.

Typically, the old religions and the theologians before Milton felt it was located within our Earth's core and that an entrance to Hell could be found. Other traditions, merely described it as an abode of the dead as with the Greek and Romans. Hell itself is often depicted abstractly, as a state of loss rather literally a detailed place of fiery torture, but this version can be traced back into the ancient and medieval tales – especially *Dante's Inferno*, Milton's

classic, and has shaped our collective as the image of fire and brimstone where the Devil rules. Almost all religions of the world detailed the opposite as a total polar opposite – up was where Christ ascended into a bright sky, to Heaven, and for the Greeks and Romans, Olympus in the cloud-shrouded mountains, and Valhalla was full of comforts for heroes, cheer, brightness, and song and endless feasting.

Bartolomeo's Map of Dantes Hell

Hel and Sheol

The word Hell itself in modern English language is derived from Old English *hel*, *helle* from Helheim, meaning the house of Hel, where the goddess who ruled the Underworld from the Anglo-Saxon (Nordic Viking) myths. This afterlife abode was a realm of a dark icy world she ruled, not a furnace of fire. In the Judeo-Christian origin of the concept Sheol, this means "The grave." In the English KJV Bible, or Gehenna, it is a separate place for those to be judged and condemned. Gehenna is mentioned in twelve references in the Bible, and this is where the raging fire is to be found. Usually, when the lake of fire is talked about, it pertains to the body being cast into it. In contrast to multiple references to Sheol and Hades, it is never mentioned that sinners being cast into it, nor is there mention of fire. From what I could gather in my research, eleven Scriptures where the word *hades* is used, and, with one exception, I find no hint of a picture of a fiery furnace. The name Gehenna is derived from Gei-Hinnom, meaning the valley of Hinnom, and in Hebrew it was called *Tophet*, which means a place of burning, for back in ancient times just outside Jerusalem there was a valley where the city's trash was hurled into a perpetually burning fire. It was said that Jesus borrowed its name in his stories in describing a raging furnace of fire, where the wicked will be cast. Paul Carus in his book, *The History of the Devil and the Idea of Evil,* writes:

THE JESUIT FATHER, CAUSSIN, THE FATHER CONFESSOR OF KING LOUIS XIII, WRITES ON HELL IN HIS BOOK, LA COUR SAINTE,—A WORK WHICH ATTAINED CONSIDERABLE FAME IN HIS DAYS, AS FOLLOWS:

"WHAT IS HELL? A SILENCE; FOR ALL THAT WHICH IS SAID OF HELL IS LESS THAN HELL ITSELF. NO JUST MAN CAN THINK OF IT WITHOUT SHEDDING THOUSANDS OF TEARS. BUT DO YOU WANT TO KNOW WHAT HELL IS? ASK TERTULLIAN. HE WILL TELL YOU THAT HELL IS A DEEP, DARK PIT OF STENCH IN WHICH ALL THE OFFAL OF THE WHOLE WORLD FLOWS TOGETHER. ASK HUGO OF ST. VICTOR. HE WILL ANSWER: 'HELL IS AN ABYSS WITHOUT A BOTTOM, WHICH OPENS THE GATES OF DESPAIR, AND WHERE ALL HOPE IS ABANDONED.' 'IT IS AN ETERNAL POOL OF FIRE,' SAYS ST. JOHN THE DIVINE (REV. XIV. 20); 'ITS AIR COMES FROM GLOWING COALS, ITS LIGHT FROM FLICKERING FLAMES. THE NIGHTS OF HELL ARE DARKNESS; THE PLACES OF REST OF THE DAMNED ARE SERPENTS AND VIPERS; THEIR HOPE IS DESPAIR. O, ETERNAL DEATH! O, LIFE WITHOUT LIFE! O, MISERY WITHOUT END!'

Duke, doctor of jurisprudence, and a learned man who was not without merit in German poetry and literature, took special interest in the mysteries of the infernal regions, and published his views in a book of 328 pages, in which he explained the tortures of the iron wheel of eternal hell torture:

"HOW MUCH TIME AND SUFFERING, HOW MUCH ANXIETY AND TORTURE OF DESPAIR, MUST BE GONE THROUGH IN HELL, MUST BE ENDURED, BORNE, EXPERIENCED AND REALIZED, BY HUNDREDS, BY THOUSANDS, BY HUNDREDS OF THOUSANDS, BY MILLIONS OF YEARS IN BURNING PITCH, IN FLAMING SULPHUR, IN RED-HOT IRON, IN POIGNANT BLOW-PIPE FLAMES, WITH WEEPING AND WAILING AND GNASHING OF TEETH INFINITE; WITH HUNGER AND THIRST MIRACULOUS; IN STENCH AND DARKNESS CRUELLY; BEFORE THIS WHEEL BE TURNED AROUND ONLY ONCE. BUT NOW THIS WHEEL OF ETERNITY IS MADE OF PURELY EVERLASTING IRON, AND MUST TURN ROUND MANY HUNDRED, YEA MILLION, AND MILLIONS OF MILLIONS OF TIMES, AND CAN NEVER WAX OLD, NEVER PERISH, NEVER BE WORN OUT, AND CAN NEVER STAND STILL IN ALL ETERNITY. "

~Justus Georg Schottel
Quoted from Paul Carus in his book:
The History of the Devil and the Idea of Evil

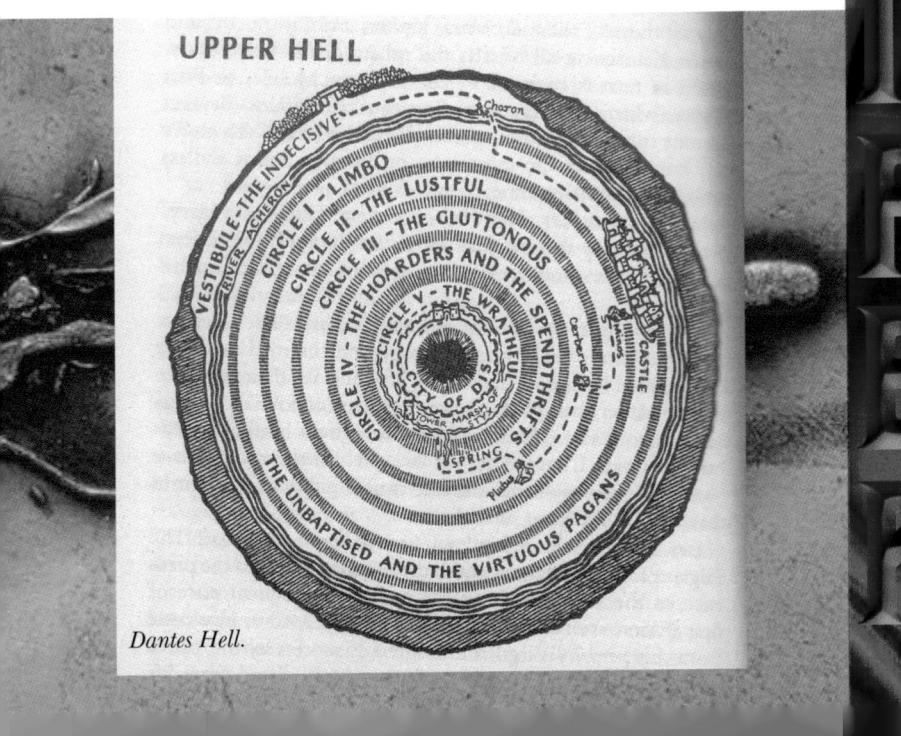

UPPER HELL

Dantes Hell.

Lucifer Balthasar Caimox.
Photo courtesy Library of
Congress.

Andreas Vesalius (December 31,
1514 - October 15, 1564).

Giotto The Last
Judgement. Fresco, dated
1304-1305.

Christ Standing on Death, Sin, and Satan,
engraving made by Crispijn de Passe the elder,
England, 1623.

Summarian

The Ancient Mesopotamians consist of Sumerians, Akkadians, Babylonians, and Assyrians, and as with all ancient mythologies, the gods live in a place in the sky in some type of Olympus heaven and most often have counter balances in their nature (sibling gods) who live in an underworld. Those such as Mot, the god of death, pestilence, and plague, ruler of the underworld, live permanently in a world without joy where there is only dust to eat and drink. From Hades and Persephone, we get the explanation of why winter fell on Earth and others tales from other religions similar with gods and goddesses who descend into the netherworld realm where they are captured and later released which causes spring.

Egyptian Land of the Dead

Discussions of hell from a Judeo–Christian perspective often exclude the Egyptian hell because it was not a permanent place of punishment. It was instead a place where the dead might be condemned after judgment by the dark gods of the underworld – this hell has Judeo-Christian elements in fire, and dismemberment, but even more so when it comes to judgment. Clearly, the influence is shown here with the Christian doctrine pulled from earlier Egyptian notions on hell that developed later in areas where Judaism has its roots. The Egyptian period covers over 1,700 years, so of course the subject of hell, given the sheer amount of time, obviously, precious little records of the Egyptians writing on the subject has survived save on inscriptions on various sarcophagi fragments of other artifacts.

Those who have withstood the test of time from c. 2705 to 1070 BCE are found within guidebooks for the dead in the otherworld and were meant for the dead to find as they were guided and protected the spirits of the dead Anubis. Lord of the Hallowed Land, as he was called, was the Egyptian god of the underworld. Anubis was depicted as black jackal-headed because the color linked him to death itself. Mummies, once embalmed became a pitch-black color. For the priests, Anubis was the deity of embalming, as well as a god of the dead. (Details on death rites of Egypt and embalming history are covered in more detail in my previous work in *Cemetery Gates: Death and Mourning through the Ages*). During funerary rituals, the priests would wear a mask of this god during the mummification process, symbolically becoming Anubis for the rituals. The Book of Amduat survived on papyrus, from the ancient necropolis of Thebes (now called Luxor) which is translated as the Book of the Hidden Room or the Book of That Which Is in the Underworld, which address the fate of the deceased; and other writing of the period mention demons found in the otherworld in a spellbook to protect the travelers.

Hortus Deliciarum, depiction of Hell
by Herrad von Landsberg Dornai.

Zoroastrianism

Zoroastrianism flourished on the Iranian plateau for 1,200 years, from the sixth century BCE to the seventh century CE and the rise of Islam in that region, and survives today among less than 200,000 faithful, mostly in India and eastern Iran. The religion is based on the teachings of Zoroaster (Zarathustra), a prophet from northeastern Iran. The consensus now is that he lived about 1200 BCE, but scholars previously argued for dates ranging from 6000 BCE until 600 BCE. Many elements that may have influenced other later emerging faiths that have extremely similar stories and characters, such as Judaism and Christianity; the surviving materials are of the time of Old Iranian pagan religions' period. The Zoroastrian transformed nearly all major beliefs in religions common around the world today such as those on the afterlife – like hell, heaven, individual judgment, and the Apocalypse. Souls would be subjected to everlasting punishment in hell, waiting thousands of years in the company of demons until centuries later they would be destroyed in the molten metal of the Apocalypse, which was then used to purify everything, so that the wicked could proceed to heaven. The afterlife begins with a three-day period after death when the soul sits at the head of its body praying for its future. After that, they are forced to cross a river that grows more difficult as their weeping relatives fill it with their tears, and at the end of the bridge is judgment from three angels called Mithra, Srosh, and Rashnu.

As for Zoroastrian hell itself, not many writings have lasted to be studied, but scholars describe a foul smelling and gloomy place in *The Book of Arda Viraf,* describing hills that are called Dush-humat, the place of evil thoughts; Dush-hukht, the place of evil words; Dush-huvarsht, the place of evil deeds; and Chakat-i-Daitih, a desert below the Chinvat Bridge, which may have been a model for bridges found later in Medieval European stories. In addition, it describes the unnamed deepest region, the pit, which is so dark it would make the punished feel as if they were all blind. *The Book of Arda Viraf* describes nearly a hundred punishments and specifies the sins that correspond with them. These punishments included a long list – they were forced to ingest and devour horrid things: their own corpses, flesh and excrement, and brains from skulls of the dead, and their own children. Other such punishments including hanging and dismemberment, decapitation, laceration, mutilation, and self-mutilation by cutting, gnawing, piercing, or are burned and cooked in ovens, cauldrons, and frying-pans, their eyes gouged out and their tongues pulled out.

Hades

Greek underworld is the term used to describe the various realms of Greek mythology which were believed to lie beneath the earth or beyond the horizon as depicted in the classic descriptions of the underworld and can be found in Homer's *Iliad* and *Odyssey*. The land of the dead ruled by the god Hades, is variously called the house or domain of Hades as well. The Elysian Fields is a place where the virtuous dead and initiates in the ancient Mysteries were sent to dwell. In order to reach the five rivers of Hades, from which the boatman Charon took coin from the dead to ferry lost souls from Styx to Acheron, the river of sorrow – which forms the boundary between upper and lower worlds.

Jahannam is the Islamic equivalent to hell, and very similar to the Hebrew word Gehinnom. Muslims who believe will be spared eternal punishment, and it details the methods of torture in Jahannam. The Qur'an states the punishments will include the burning of skin, only to be healed so that it can be burned off again. First, however, their skin and internal organs are scalded with boiling water, their faces will be scraped as sinners are dragged along fire, bound in yokes then dragged through boiling water and fire. Not surprisingly, the majority of hell's inhabitants were women who were ungrateful to their husbands. The Qur'an says: "Like dregs of oil; it shall boil in (their) bellies, Like the boiling of hot water." Islamic sources indicate that all evil creatures, both human and jinn (including Satan himself) will be tormented by the angel Maalik.

Hinduism

The early Vedic religion did not have a concept of Hell, but later Hindu books do mention a realm similar to Hell, called Naraka Hell that is also described in various other scriptures. *The Garuda Purana* gives a detailed account of Hell, its features and enlists amounts of punishment for most of the crimes, similar to our modern-day penal code. Judged by the god Yamarāja, who is also the god of death, reigns over Hell, punishments include dipping in boiling oil, burning in fire, and torture using various weapons. Individuals who finish their quota of the punishments are reborn in accordance with their balance of karma.

Buddism

Buddhist texts described hell as a segmented place where sinners will be punished in specific ways for specific sins, and move from hell to hell before rebirth. As with other aspects, the Buddhist ideas of hell, are like so much else coming from the Hinduism faith. While the surviving texts vary somewhat in naming the Buddhist hells, the earliest examples say that Buddhist hell was conceived of as a series of eight hells, one above the other, each with sixteen secondary hells, four at each of the four gates of the great hells – or 136 hells in total. Tibetan traditions add another eight major hells, layering eight cold hells above the eight standard hot hells, all having sixteen secondary hells or 272 hells.

Chinese texts mentions the necropolis in Fengdu, the sculpture gardens at Baodingshan, and the Beijing Temple of the Eighteen Hells, described simply First Court of Hell, Second Court of Hell, and so on. The first court is actually a place of judgment on the life ends, and the tenth, a place for reassignment to the new life about to begin. The eight others offer punishments for different sins, and hell serves as a place of purgation, where individuals suffer for periods of time, before they are reborn. When nearly dead, they are revived and the process goes on for countless years, in which each day is equal to 30,000 earthly years. Souls are sentenced to this hell for 80,000 years or 1,800 billion years. *The Sutra on the Eighteen Hells* describes the length of suffering in one hell: A place is red hot iron so the people are burned and are boiled until their flesh drops off. The range of sins punished in hell is much greater in Buddhism, where each rebirth is expected to be a further step along the path to enlightenment. The punishments range from torture and dismemberment, drowning, burning, and crushing await the damned to sharp objects of all sorts, chains, pincers, thorns, and axes, and attacks by all manner of animals, birds, snakes, and maggots.

The earliest man held the belief that Hell was an underworld which spans many cultures and cross continents for generations. It was adapted by future generations as religion changed due to the fact that man created his fears of deep dark places – where the dead go from burial onward, further down spiritually made sense. Like death, the dark is unknowing and what we fear, we shy away from. Hell and its particulars had become such an accepted place in all faiths, as long as man walked the Earth everywhere, had been developed and shaped by man himself, stretched to the limits of imagination, even in films such as *Spawn*, *Hellraiser*, *Drag me to Hell*, and so many others to this day. It is unlikely to ever pin down the exact location from even the most educated theologian in times past or present. Indeed, even during the Age of Reason rebukes were made ever more prominent as science began to cause skepticism, as men such as Thomas Paine began to ridicule the idea. Many free thinkers said pain was man's greatest evil, not sin, and universal good and truth were not possible. Man started to see things as tangible and real or intangible equating to fantasy.

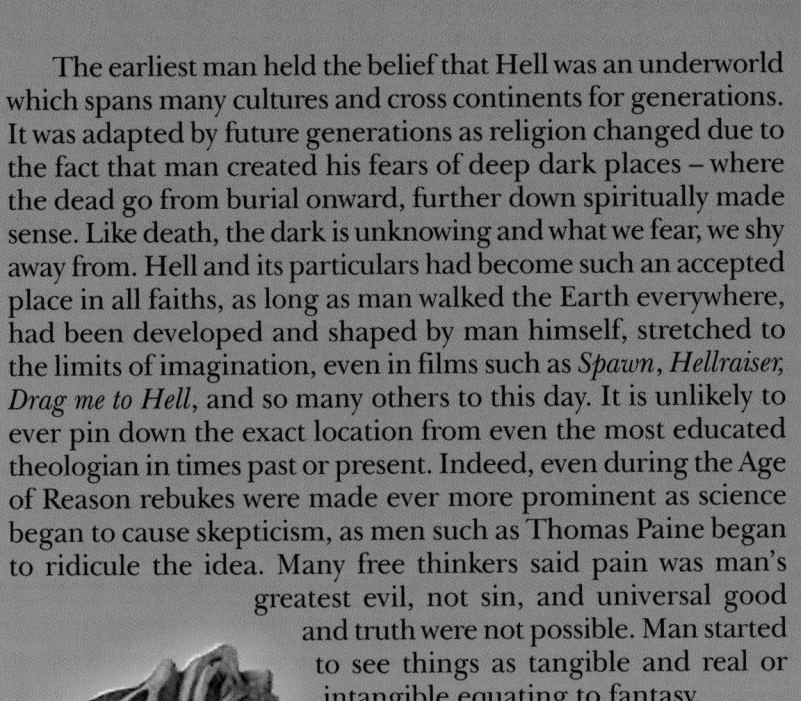

Asian Demon, artist unknown

Chapter Three

The Devil's Champions

"What! Can the Devil speak true?"

~ Shakespeare
Macbeth

As science and secular thinking grew beyond the reach of the power and control of religion, even the religious free thinkers began to question the exact nature of the archfiend. Revolutionary and heretical propositions were brought to the forefront of the public, whether hidden metaphorically or blatantly in art, poetry, and major literary works.

Great Red Dragon Blake (1806-1809). Photo courtesy Library of Congress.

The Devil in the Age of Enlightenment

Not since Niccoli Machiavelli wrote his satire on the Devil in the late 1550s did the common man begin to take a stand – that is, until the Age of Reason. Thinkers of great renown came to shake up and hold sway over people in ways that previously only clergy had. Pragmatists holding dear to revolutionary ideas of Voltaire, Isaac Newton, and many other secular Humanists during the eighteenth and nineteenth centuries further challenged the idea of the Devil, boldly using satire in the writings and art, blasphemously going so far as to invert the enemy status of Lucifer in literature, sometimes using him as an example of virtues that Christianity denied, such as pride and lust that has carried over into Satanism of our day. As speakers shouted their logic, no skies darkened with biblical plague locusts while man denounced God, Satan, nor any other spiritual realities. With skepticism of cynics, the Devil at last was shown to have only the collective value men were willing to give over to it. I recommend reading *The Devil and Secular Humanism: The Children of the Enlightenment*, by Howard B. Radest.

Early Plays and Literature

In popular literature, the Devil has been much more than an incarnation of pure evil. He is the figure that tweaks us on the nose when life is too serious, he inspires man to desire more out of life than we would settle for without him, and instills in us the desire to grow intellectually – as the key idealist of the spirit of progress, as evident in the great classic *Faust*, where man sought knowledge above even the usefulness of his own soul.

Voltaire

The original Voltaire's birth name was François-Marie Arouet de Voltaire. Not to be confused with the modern-day singer of Project Records, who took his name from the rebel in history. He was born into a middle class family, on November 21, 1694, in Paris, France. He was a writer, satirist, the embodiment of the eighteenth-century Enlightenment, remembered as a crusader against tyranny and bigotry. Voltaire was educated by the Jesuits at the Collège Louis-le-Grand. He studied law and then worked as a secretary to the French ambassador in Holland before devoting himself entirely to writing. He energetically attacked the government and the Catholic Church, which earned him numerous imprisonments and exiles. In 1716 Voltaire was arrested and exiled from Paris for five months. From 1717 to 1718, he found himself imprisoned in the Bastille for lampooning of the Regency. During this time, he wrote the tragedy Œdipe, and started to use the name Voltaire. The play brought him fame, but also more enemies at court.

Voltaire. Photo courtesy Library of Congress.

Voltaire lived at the Château de Cirey with Madame du Châtelet in 1734-36 and 1737-40. In 1755, he settled in Switzerland, where he lived the rest of his life, apart from trips to France. As an essayist, Voltaire defended freedom of thought and religious tolerance. His famous saying, "I wholly disapprove of what you say, but will defend to the death your right to say it" marked his attitude in life. In true Humanistic style, he believed humanity was far from its state of freedom and perfection. His *Dictionnaire Philosphique* (1764) was condemned in Paris, Geneva, and Amsterdam, and for safety reasons, Voltaire denied his authorship. He did, however, in 1760, publicly become a Deist to everyone.

Voltaire died in Paris on May 30, 1778, at 84, the undisputed leader of the Age of Enlightenment. In the Golden Age of Enlightenment, he left behind over 14,000 known letters and over 2,000 books and pamphlets, and to Humanists, perhaps one of the most famous of the Devil's advocates.

The Theosophical Society, founded in New York in 1875, was an occult and mystical order that endeavored to create a brotherhood of man, and had a sympathetic view of Lucifer. They saw him as a personification of independence. Such mystical schools often taught that Lucifer's fall was merely a fable to use as an analogy for the journey of the mind as members become aware of their reality as separate beings in order to gain the knowledge of their unique identity. Lucifer is seen as the archetypal will within humans to break free of dogma and established forms and live life on their own terms, says Seth Mullins, author of *Song of the Twice Born, Book I: The Mirror of Sirrus*.

Eliphas Levi, an occultist of the early 1900s, saw some good in the figure of Satan, which he identified with the forces of "generation," a euphemism for sex. The Golden Dawn also came to see Satan or the Devil as a necessary counterpoint to God. Aleister Crowley embraced this trend more thoroughly, identifying Satan with one of his primary deities. In popular culture, the "Satanic school" turned into the decadent movement, exemplified by Lord Byron and Baudelaire. We'll look into all of this to further explain my points.

If the Devil never existed, humanity certainly felt the need to create one, as evidence in all the stories we love to read, movies we watch, and in the plays penned centuries ago. Lucifer has been the subject of a vast number of writers who show him even in comic books as he tempts man into doing our most sordid and wickedness, all the while doing as the writer Baudelaire says in *The Generous Gambler*, "The loveliest trick of the Devil is to persuade you that he does not exist!"

Goethe's Faust

One of the more interesting aspects of Satan is the recurring theme of humans making a pact with the Devil. The Faust legend is this: In exchange for one's soul, Satan will grant the human summoner with wealth or power for a specified time. In most versions of the story, Faust tricks the Devil and avoids punishment, unlike the original where the Devil kills and mutilates Faust at the end. His brains are splattered on the walls of his room, his eyes and teeth lie on the floor, and his corpse is left to rot.

Classics works *Faust* and *The Tragical History of Doctor Faustus* feature the demon known as Mephistopheles, (also spelled Mephistophilius), called from Hell by Faust to trade up his soul for years of pleasure.

In the film adaptation called *Faust*, the Devil goes by the name Mephisto. Unlike the other two Devils, Mephisto had three different appearances and each appearance came the closest to looking like our stereo typical pop-culture Devil than that of the other versions. In *Faust*, Mephisto takes the form of an old human with some demonic features including a tail. Of the three films, *Faust* was the only film where horns and tails appeared.

Goethe

Faust 1887 Theatrical Poster Collection.

ON AS "MEPHISTOPHELES"

AUST!

DICKMAN, JONES & HETTRICH, SAN FRANCISCO.

Paradise Lost

The great English poet William Blake said that the scribe John Milton's epic poem was proof he was in league with the Devil, and, rightly so that his antihero was much more like his audience. Flawed, full of human imperfections, pride, and due to the fact he embodies what our modern culture prizes most; our fierce independent Lucifer is the archetype of archetypes of rebellion and free will.

John Milton

John Milton was born on December 9, 1608, in London. Milton's father was also a composer of church music, and Milton himself experienced a lifelong delight in music. The family's financial prosperity afforded Milton to be taught classical languages, first by private tutors at home, followed by entrance to St. Paul's School at age 12, in 1620. In 1625, Milton admitted to Christ's College, Cambridge. While

Lucifer Dore 1887.

Milton was a hardworking student, he was also argumentative to the extent that only a year later, in 1626, he got suspended after a dispute with his tutor, William Chappell. During his temporary return to London, Milton attended plays, and perhaps began his first forays into poetry.

At his return to Cambridge, Milton was assigned a new tutor, Nathaniel Tovey. Life at Cambridge was still not easy on Milton; he felt he was disliked by many of his fellow students and he was dissatisfied with the curriculum. In April 1637, Milton was nearing the end of his studies when his mother died and was buried at Horton. Around 1632, Milton took his M.A. *cum laude* at Cambridge, after which he retired to the family homes in London and Horton, Buckinghamshire, for years of private study and literary composition.

Milton arrived in Florence; then found Galileo arrested and on house arrest by order of the Inquisition. In Rome, he was a guest of Cardinal Barberini, the Pope's nephew, and visited the Vatican Library. Milton's tour of Europe was cut short with rumors of impending civil war in England, and he returned home in July 1634. He spent his time tutoring students while finishing his life's work, the epic, *Paradise Lost*. This epic saga finally saw publication in 1667, in a set of ten books.

In *Paradise Lost*, Satan acts much like a protagonist in the first half of the story, who styles himself as an ambitious underdog rebelling against Heaven. "The Protestant Devil," says Paul Carus, "received his finishing touches from Milton...acquires nobility of soul, moral strength, independence and manliness..." Satan is readily comparable to the heroes of the classical epics – this "hero," Satan, contains elements of the hero in classical tragedy, complete with his fatal flaw which is his lack of self-knowledge. He has no ability to recognize his own limitations. He in no way seems to realize that he can never win in a contest between the Creator and the created being. Satan goes from "reign[ing] in Hell" in Book I to his final appearance in Book X where he is transformed into a "monstrous Serpent" by the power of God reaching into Hell. Like a typical Greek tragedy, the play by Milton portrays his tragic lead a metaphor for the ultimate hero, or

Dore's *Satan trapped in Hell 1887.*
Courtesy of Library of Congress.

in this case, sinner. Out of stubbornness, he adamantly refuses the offer of forgiveness and salvation. Milton's Satan is arguably the hero of his epic poem and that appears to be Milton's intent, achieving an epic antihero second to none before or after in literature.

A Devil of a Problem: Satan as Hero in Paradise Lost, by Matt Wallace remarks on Gods use of free will:

...FREE WILL DEFENSE TO THE PROBLEM OF EVIL FAILS DUE TO THE
INTERNAL CONTRADICTIONS IN THE CHRISTIAN GOD. IF EVERYTHING
THAT EXISTS COMES FROM AN ALL-POWERFUL AND ALL-KNOWING
GOD, HOW CAN EVIL EXIST WITHIN THE CREATION OF AN ALL-GOOD
GOD? HOW CAN SATAN AND HIS REBEL ANGELS EXIST? THE ULTIMATE
FAILURE OF THE FREE WILL DEFENSE LIES IN THE FACT THAT GOD IS THE
PROXIMATE CAUSE OF EVERYTHING THAT EXISTS, AND EVERYTHING EXISTS
AS IT DOES PRECISELY BECAUSE GOD WILLED IT SO. GOD CREATED ALL
THAT EXISTS, AND HE DID SO WITH FULL KNOWLEDGE OF THE NATURE
AND THE ULTIMATE FATE OF ALL HIS CREATIONS. EVEN IF ONE ALLOWS
KNOWLEDGE AND CHOICE WITHIN SENTIENT BEINGS AND HOLDS THEM
ACCOUNTABLE FOR THEIR DECISIONS, THERE IS ONE DECISION THAT
WAS NEVER THEIRS: THE DECISION TO EXIST IN THE FIRST PLACE. ...
MILTON'S SOUNDS LIKE NOTHING MORE THAN A PETTY THEOLOGIAN.
UNFORTUNATELY AND TERRIFYINGLY, MILTON'S GOD HAS ULTIMATE
KNOWLEDGE AND ULTIMATE POWER, AND MILTON PORTRAYS HIM
CAPRICIOUSLY USING AND NOT USING BOTH. THOUGH HE CLEARLY
COULD DO OTHERWISE, HE CREATES WITH FULL AWARENESS OF THE
FLAWS WITHIN HIS CREATIONS AND ALLOWS THEM TO ACT ON THEIR
FLAWS. WHEN HIS CREATIONS FAIL AS A CONSEQUENCE OF THE FLAWS
HE KNOWINGLY INCORPORATED INTO THEM, HE PUNISHES THEM FOR
WHAT IS ULTIMATELY HIS FAULT AND FAILURE AS CREATOR.

Though Milton actually intended his Satan as a mockery of
sin and evil, he created a character so real and so human that one
can't help but be drawn to him – this work influenced the modern
archetype of the Devil as a noble, misunderstood hero (very like
Ann Rice's character Lestat, which is the likely reason Memnoch
picks Lestat as his right-hand man in *Memnoch the Devil*!). Arguably,
Paradise Lost is among the greatest works ever written in English.
Even more remarkable for Milton's blindness – he would compose
verse upon verse at night in his head and then dictate them from
memory to his aides in the morning. This work contains the Devil's
famous line, "Better to reign in Hell than serve in Heaven," used in
the old *Star Trek* episode which showed the eugenic superman who
became better known in the film, *The Wrath of Khan*. It influenced
C. S. Lewis with *The Screwtape Letters*. It was a strong influence
on Shelley's *Frankenstein*, as we see in the introduction where
the monster in *Prometheus Unbound*, he attempts to understand
humanity. The creature thinks of himself as Satan in comparison
to Vicktor as God. "Evil henceforth become my good," he says.
Blake's point begins to make sense if *Paradise Lost* is evaluated on
its poetic success and its theological failure.

In his masterpiece, *The Screwtape Letters*, C. S. Lewis imagines
Hell as a gruesome bureaucracy. This book was made into a play
dramatization, and has an appearance by award-winning actor Andy
Serkis ("Gollum" in *Lord of the Rings*) and also stars Geoffrey Palmer,
Laura Michelle Kelly, Eileen Page, and other world-class actors.

William Blake

William Blake was a bit of a late Renaissance man, though largely ignored during his lifetime. Born in London in 1757, he was a pioneer in the Decadent period, around the same time as Sir Francis Dashwood. He was a poet, artist, a visionary mystic, and engraver (who illustrated and printed his own books, centuries before vanity press existed in its current form!). Blake is important to note among writers linked to esoteric thinkers as he used mysticism as inspiration in his work, despite the fact he proclaimed the supremacy of the imagination over the rationalism of the eighteenth century. Misunderstanding dogged his career as a writer and artist. It was not until generations passed until many would recognize his importance – I recently ran across his name in Anne Rice's *Memnoch the Devil*, where the statue of a fallen angel was said to resemble that of Blake's artwork. In 1767, he was sent to Henry Pars' drawing school. Blake has recorded that from his early years, he experienced visions of angels (while sitting nude in a treetop as a youth) and ghostly monks. He claimed to have seen and conversed with the angel, Gabriel, the Virgin Mary, and various historical figures. No doubt, that fact influenced Rice's use of his name. Blake said of Milton, "He was a true Poet and of the Devil's party without knowing it."

At the age of 14, Blake apprenticed for several years to an engraver, and his work became influenced further by Gothic art and architecture. Blake's first book of poems, *Poetical Sketches*, appeared in 1783 and he followed it by *Songs of Innocence* some time later. Interestingly, I discovered that Allen Ginsberg nearly convinced Mick Jagger to redo this work in a song, according to Gavin Baddeley's research in *Lucifer Rising*. In the ending of the Rice film, *Interview with a Vampire*, the song *Sympathy for the Devil* is an obvious tribute to the Stones version by Guns and Roses singer Axel Rose. We'll look into Satan and rock and roll later on. The anti-hero connection of the Decadents again is subtly felt once more mixing the anti-hero vampire archetype with Milton's Devil.

In *Songs of Innocence*, the world is seen from a child's point of view, but they also function as tales relevant to the adult experience. Blake engraved and published most of his major works himself. Famous among his *Prophetic Books* are *The Book of Thel*, *The Marriage of Heaven and Hell*, *The Book of Urizen*, *America*, *Milton*, and *Jerusalem*. In his *Prophetic Books*, Blake expressed his constant concern with the struggle of the soul to free its "natural energies from reason and organized religion." Among Blake's later art works are drawings and engravings for Dante's *Divine Comedy* that did not see completion until he was nearly 70 years old. Blake died on August 12, 1827, and was buried in an unmarked grave in a public cemetery. Though generally thought of as an eccentric during his own life, as time passed, he is highly rated as both a poet and artist.

William Blake's
version of Lucifer

William Blake's
version of
Dante's Hell.
Courtesy Library
of Congress.

Dante's Inferno

Unlike Goethe tragedy, *Divine Comedy* was closer to a comedy, focusing on the human situation and showed our frailties and fundamental flaws. The *Divine Comedy* (or, as it was originally *published in 1555 Italy as*, *Divina Commedia*) is the epic poem written by Dante Alighieri, and is considered one of the greatest works of world literature. The poem's imaginative and allegorical vision of the afterlife speculated during the medieval period helped the Church developed it further in the minds of people from then onward.

On the surface, the poem describes Dante's travels through Hell, Purgatory, and Heaven, and is divided into three parts, the *Inferno*, *Purgatorio*, and *Paradiso*. The poem is written in the first person, and tells of Dante's journey through the three realms of the dead. The Roman poet, Virgil, guides him through Hell and Purgatory; and then he is guided through Heaven. This work draws on what was common knowledge in the Medieval Christian theology and philosophy, especially the writings of Thomas Aquinas Dante, representing an allegory for the soul's journey towards God.

This classic has been a source of inspiration for countless artists for seven centuries. There are many references to Dante's work in literature, and in art the famous sculptor Auguste Rodin was inspired by themes from Dante, and many visual artists have illustrated Dante's work, as shown in the illustrations by Dore. There have also been many references to the *Divine Comedy* in cinema and computer games.

The third circle, illustration from *Dante's Inferno* by Stradanus.

Charles Baudelaire

France's best poet, who lived in the 1800s, believed in the existence of the Devil, the sordid nature of humanity and wrote *The Generous Gambler* in 1864, a story where the Devil is a Paris man who gambles for peoples souls. Charles Baudelaire was a nineteenth-century Decadent. The French poet, translator, and literary and art critic's reputation rests primarily on *Les Fleurs du mal, The Flowers of Evil* – perhaps the most important and influential poetry collection published in Europe in the nineteenth century. Similarly, his 1868 *Little Prose Poems* was the most successful and innovative early experiment in prose poetry of the time. Known for his controversial and often dark poetry, as well as his translation of the tales of Edgar Allan Poe, Baudelaire's life was filled with drama and anguish, mostly due to financial problems while being prosecuted for his works deemed as obscenity and blasphemy. He was quoted as saying once, "All literature is the consequence of sin." In his often-introspective poetry, Baudelaire revealed himself as a seeker of God without religious beliefs, and sought every manifestation of life for some kind of true significance. Like the gloomier Poe, Baudelaire crafted works mixing decay with beauty, in true Gothic style showing in death to be the reason to cherish life – the reason why antiquity Goths of the 1980s and 90s were originally called New Decadents, long before renaming themselves "Goths."

Baudelaire began his education at the Collège Royal in Lyons. It was during this time that Baudelaire began to show promise as a student and a writer. Intense melancholy also developed and the poet was expelled, in 1839, from school due to his consistent acts of indiscipline. Eventually, Baudelaire became a nominal student, while living a "free life" in the Latin Quarter, where he made his first contacts in the literary world, and contracted the venereal disease that eventually would take his life. Baudelaire jumped a ship in Mauritius and ultimately made his way back to France in February of 1842. The voyage and his exploits after jumping the ship enriched his imagination, and brought a rich mixture of exotic images to his works. He wrote of the Devil once: "This just shows," he once remarked, "that the Devil does not scorn imbeciles but makes good use of them, to do his work for him…. The Devil pulls the strings which make us dance; we find delight in the most loathsome things; some furtherance of Hell each new day brings, and yet we feel no horror in that rank advance."

Baudelaire received an inheritance the same year and rapidly proceeded to dissipate it on the lifestyle of a true Gothic dandy,

Charles Baudelaire, 1863.
Courtesy Library of Congress.

spending freely on the finest clothes, books, works of art, expensive food and wines, and, as rumor has it, opium. Baudelaire's extravagance exhausted half his fortune in less than two years, and he fell prey to banks and other debts, thus laying the foundation for huge debts that would haunt him for the rest of his life. His family levied on him a legal arrangement that restricted his access to his inheritance. A minuscule allowance barely granted him enough to clear his debts, causing him emotional and financial dependence on his mother while increasing his growing resentment for his stepfather. The moods of isolation and despair that Baudelaire had known in adolescence became more frequent. However, to this day he remains to this day a renowned poet and critic.

Washington Irving

In *The Devil and Daniel Webster,* the Devil is called Mr. Scratch, and in the film adaptation had just one manifestation as a white male in his fifties by actor Walter Huston. He had slanted bushy eyebrows, side burns, and a twinkle in eye that gave him a definitive Devilish look. The Devil put two pennies in Jabez's pocket the moment Jabez Stone spoke of selling his soul for two cents. After Jabez signed the contract on his soul, his situation improved drastically. Other examples of good luck followed, such as, after the storm, Jabez was able to hire those men whose crops were destroyed, and in seven years, Jabez became a banker. He began to dress more extravagantly, took a mistress (a gift from Scratch) and built a mansion down the lane from his modest old house where his mother and wife remained. Jabez transformed from a friendly farmer into a greedy capitalist.

At the end, Daniel Webster, a lawyer and politician, saved Jabez's soul by appealing to the jury's idea of American freedom. Mr. Scratch lost and Jabez went back to being a friendly farmer who once again embraced rural American values. This story no doubt influenced *The Devils Advocate*, as did *Faust* before Irving's story.

Edgar Allen Poe

Perhaps the most recognized writer of horror before Stephen King was Poe who wrote classics like *The Raven*, *The Tell-Tale Heart*, *The Cask of Amontillado*, and *The Masque of the Red Death*. The story *Bon-Bon* from 1835 features Old Scratch speaking to a philosopher conversing on the Epicurean delights Satan finds intriguing in us, and *in The Devil in the Belfry* we find a satirical short story published in 1839 that pokes fun at the notion that all literature should have a moral and spoofs transcendentalism. The Devil character is a troublemaker who destroys the serenity of tradition. Poe mocks the town's ridiculous traditions, proving metaphorically the Devil serves to inspire originality and creativity in an otherwise stagnant environment.

J.Sheridan Le Fanu

Known most of all for "Carmilla," the first vampire lesbian erotica story ever done, J. Sheridan Le Fann wrote a story about the Devil in 1872 called "Sir Dominick's Bargain" based off an Irish legend. During the Victorian time period, Le Fanu was one of the originators of modern psychological horror novels.

Friedrich Nietzsche

In the year 1844, a German philosopher was born. Friedrich Nietzsche refuted the worship of religion in general and any system that undermines the individuality of the human. In 1888, he published a book and assumed the mantle of the Anti-Christ. Friedrich saw himself as heralding the death of Christianity and Christian morality. When you think of Satan the way Nietzsche did, he could represent the elevation of the individualists own ego and not an anthropomorphic creature with horns, hooves, and tail which is looked upon only as a symbol.

Nietzsche held fast to the theory that evil was a relative concept. This was a fairly new theory on people, outside that of Auguste Comte, who upon the materialistic basis of Positivism, founded the religion of humanity, and professed to substitute an enthusiasm for humanity as the motive for socially correct action, over those that were righteous – or of supernatural and religious. *Der Antichrist*, translated as *The Anti-Christian*, was published in 1895.

Nietzsche expressed his dissatisfaction with modernity. He disliked the "contemporary lazy ...cowardly compromise, tolerance," and "resignation." Nietzche was most famous for his ideas on how man is in reality, void of denial to himself and his wants – a devilishly proud trait, as he introduced his concept of "will to power," as he defined the concepts of "good, bad, and happiness" in relation to the will to power. "What is good? — All that heightens the feeling of power, the will to power, power itself in man. What is bad? — All that proceeds from weakness. What is happiness? — The feeling that power *increases,* that a resistance is overcome.... *Not* contentment, but more power; *not* peace at all, but war ..." Mankind, according to Nietzsche, is corrupt and its highest values are depraved. He asserted that "... all the values in which mankind at present summarizes its highest desiderata are *decadence values.*" He hated wishful thinking and proclaimed it a waste of one's life and productivity. The Ubermensch was the "superman" that is, the ultimate that human potential could reach if only we shook off the shackles of the dogmatic oppression of religion and self doubt. This is one of the hallmarks of modern Satanism, as we will explore the religion (in a large part based from Nietzsche). He felt mankind was depraved because it had lost its instincts and prefers what was harmful to it. "I consider life itself instinct for growth, for durability, for accumulation of forces, for *power*: Where the will to power is lacking there is decline."

Christianity, as the religion of pity, was despised by Nietzsche, as pity leads to depression, loss of vitality and strength, and is harmful to ones will or life. Pity also preserves that which should naturally be destroyed, such as the weak, and sick people, whose will to power has declined. Nietzsche opposed the Christian concept of God because it "... degenerated into the *contradiction of life*, instead of being life's transfiguration" and, he felt very strongly that the Christian God is a antagonistic to mans true nature. In his words, God is to him a "... declaration of war against life, against nature, against the will to live!" Faith and belief are opposed to reason, knowledge, and inquiry, he believed. Hope, to him, in the Beyond sustains the unhappy multitudes. *The Antichrist* is not intended to refer to the biblical Satan, but is rather an attack on what he called *slave morality* of Christianity. Nietzsche's basic claim is that Christianity (as he saw it in the West) is a poisoner of western culture. And he saw Christianity as a

dominate illusion. His writing *God is Dead* was an outcry that God was not really dead, rather on his deathbed, and soon would disappear from the thoughts of man. The provocative title is mainly expressing Nietzsche's animus toward Christianity, as such. In this book, Nietzsche is very critical of institutionalized religion. As an opponent to major themes found in Judeo-Christianity, most people felt he was truly of the Devil to be inspired to such blasphemy.

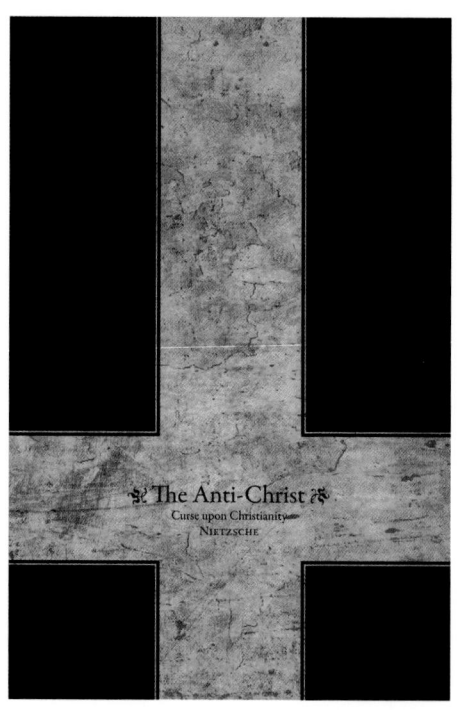

Nietzsche The Antichrist. Courtesy Underworld Amusements, 2009.

Friedrich Willhelm Nietzsche 1882. *Courtesy Library of Congress.*

The Devils presented in each film was appropriate for their time – Mephisto had an exaggerated look and sweeping gestures fit the film's genre. German Expressionism and the future filmmakers in turn gave their evil entity a unique image in their films, which represented a time span that started in 1926 and went through to 1997. It was fascinating to watch that image evolve over time. Appearance, power, and actions all contributed to the image of the Devil.

We'll briefly look at the most recognized and influential of them, from Faust to Nicholson, and Pacino in *The Devil's Advocate*.

Rosemary's Baby

The (1968) Polish director Roman Polanski's first American feature film and his second scary horror film – following his first disturbing film in English titled *Repulsion* (1965) – about a mentally-unstable, sexually-terrified woman (Catherine Deneuve) left alone in her apartment. *Rosemary's Baby* is a classic from the year 1968 story-turned-film by infamous director Romna Ploanski, about a young newlywed couple who moves into a large and slightly foreboding old apartment building in Central Park West, after their honeymoon. They become friendly with Rosemary, who is a young and naive housewife played by Mia Farrow, whose actor husband, played by John Cassavetes, arranges with members of a coven to have his wife impregnated by the Devil in exchange for success in a Broadway play. Rosemary's pregnancy seems normal and happy in this moment in her life until she grows increasingly suspicious of her eccentric next-door neighbors' influence. The director cleverly made it so that the viewer is never quite certain whether Rosemary's nightmarish experiences, such as her dream of making love to Satan, are truly real or mere hallucinations. Rosemary says that her infant son "has his father's eyes" in a voice over.

Polanski's film received two Academy Award nominations, one for Best Adapted Screenplay and actress Ruth Gordon received the Best Supporting Actress award. It has been debated for decades that The Church of Satan founder, Anton LaVey, wore the Devil costume during the sex scene, clad in a demonic rubber suit. In 1971, this suit was acquired by Studio One Productions in Louisville, Kentucky, for use in a low-budget horror film *Asylum of Satan*. Anton LaVey was called on for his expertise by Polanski for his advice on Satanic rites, and he later make an appearance at the San Francisco opening of the film. Anton LaVey's remark to him later lauded the film as "a breakthrough in the portrayal of real Satanists," Polanski said, quoting from memory in his biography.

This would later lead to wild accusations of "orgies, drug parties and black magic" after the murder of his wife Sharon by the Manson Family on August 9th 1969.

The Mephisto Waltz

The Mephisto Waltz is a 1971 American horror film/murder mystery, directed by Paul Wendkos and starred Alan Alda, Jacqueline Bisset, Barbara Parkins. This movie is taken from the piano work by Franz List of the same name, composed in 1859 through 1885. The film centers around of a version of Faust. Myles Clarkson, long ago frustrated in his hope for a career as a pianist, is now a music journalist and interviews Duncan Ely, a great virtuoso. Duncan soon takes notice that she is nearly perfect for the piano. From that point, Duncan (as Duncan's physical body) nears its end, father and daughter perform an occult ritual which transfers Duncan's consciousness into Myles's body. Myles's ensuing change in personality, which includes his now being able to play the piano as well as had Duncan, is noticed by Paula, but she is initially unsuspecting of the cause. Though confused by the change in her husband, she also finds his new persona exciting and attractive. Later, Paula transfers her own consciousness into Roxanne's body, leaving her own body to be found as a suicide. Paula returns in Roxanne's body, to Duncan/Myles, telling her of Paula's suicide, never to reveal herself.

The Devil's Rain

The Devil's Rain is a 1975 low-budget horror film, one of several B-films William Shatner starred in between the original *Star Trek* television series and the *Star Trek* movies. It also starred Tom Skerritt, Ernest Borgnine, Eddie Albert, and Keenan Wynn. As in Polanski works, the High Priest of the Church of Satan, Anton LaVey, is credited as the films technical advisor on this tale about a curse hovering over the Preston family, caused by their betrayal of the Satanic priest John Corbis, played by Ernest Borgnine. Mark Preston, William Shatner's character, takes the book, hoping to meet with Corbis and defeat him, in a ghost town in the desert. *The Devil's Rain* received a uniformly negative critical response, with the chief complaint being the incoherent story line. The film's refusal to provide adequate scares was also widely criticized.

The Devil Rides Out

Hammer Film Productions released *The Devil Rides Out* in 1968, based off of the original 1934 novel by Dennis Wheatley with the same title about black magic and the occult. Followers of Satan attempt to sacrifice the niece of the Duke of Richeleau, played by Christopher Lee. Lee himself often stated that of all his vast work in films, this is his favorite and the one he would like to see remade with modern special effects. The actors of this epic, battle the forces of Richleau from black magic (The Duc de Richeleau). His friend, Rex, discovers their young charge, Simon, has fallen in with the powers of Darkness and is about to be baptized into the service of evil. The Duc is fortunately versed in such matters and finds himself locked in a duel with the deadly Mocata, disciple of the left-hand path.

An interesting story and, of course, acted well by Lee; but other than stereotyping the popular imaginations of movie attendees on black magic and Devil worship, this movie didn't have a huge impact on how the Devil was perceived.

The Omen

In 1976, Richard Donner directed the classic tale featuring a little boy named Damien, son of an American diplomat, starring Gregory Peck as the father, Robert Thorn of Damien, played by Harvey Stephens, and his wife, living in London. The wife turns out to be marked with the sign of Satan, the infamous 666. Lee Remick, who played his wife, Katherine Thorn, has much less of a role in the film. Kathy has been mentally stressed by Damien. After her to visit a therapist, Katherine tells Robert she wants to have an abortion. Disturbed by the news, Thorn makes a trip to see the therapist – however, on his way back, Kathy has an accident that causes her to miscarry. It soon becomes apparent that Damien could be the Anti-Christ incarnate. I would suggest to my readers to watch both the original and the remake and decide for themselves which is the better of the two.

This movie has been referenced in everything from *South Park* to *Rosanne,* and countless other films and sitcoms. I recall on the film was infamously released on June 6, 2006, at 06:06:06 in the morning. This symbolically represents the number 666, the biblical "Number of the Beast" and attended the midnight showing myself of the 2006 remake Liev Schreiber as Robert Thorn, Julia Stiles as his wife, Katherine, and young Seamus Davey-Fitzpatrick as Damien. Directed by John Moore and written by David Seltzer, with several adjustments in the retelling, such as when Mrs. Baylock dies when Robert stabs her in the neck and shoulder with kitchen utensils in the original. Here, he runs her over with his car, in the original ending in both the book and original film. This is in *The Omen: 666*, which is featured as a deleted scene in the 30th Anniversary DVD edition, but I found the ending quite well done, with Robert driving to a church to kill Damien on consecrated ground. Right as he is about to kill the child with the sacred knife, he is killed by an officer (sniper) of the Diplomatic Protection Group. At the funeral for Robert at the end of the remake, we see the President of the United States holding the hand of Damien who slowly turns to stare at the viewer and slowly gives a chilling smile.

Legend

In 1985, we are presented with *Legend,* a film from 20th Century Fox and Universal Pictures. Ridley Scott (*Blade Runner*) starred along with the up-and-coming Tom Cruise who plays Jack; his love interest is Mia Sara who plays Lili in a tale of the classic struggle between Good and Evil in broad allegorical terms. It depicts the struggle between Darkness, a horned demon played masterfully by Tim Curry, who plans to disperse eternal night in the land where this story takes place, by killing every unicorn in the world. The demon seeks to create eternal night by destroying the last of the unicorns and marrying a fairy princess. Although he looks unbeatable, Jack, a forest boy played by a very young Tom Cruise, along with his friends, bravely tries to save the world and princess Lili (the intended and unwilling bride) from the Darkness.

In my opinion, Curry's performance is the best reason to see this movie. His Devil is intelligent, powerful, and ambitious, yet all the same he is tragic, for he longs for Lili to love him. Echoing sentiments of Milton's Satan, "...in madness lies the soul of all that's noble....can you fathom the loneliness of untold eons lived in darkness? My spirit was forged in that black fire." The film's original title, *Legend of Darkness*, hinted that screenwriter William Hjortsberg found *Darkness* more interesting than any of the other facets of the movie, including the people, reminiscent of Milton using Satan as his focal point. In my mind, this is one of the best special effects for how the classic Devil was said to appear. It has become such a cult classic. Satan (Darkness) has even been made into a collector's figurine in the fifth film by Movie Maniacs' line from McFarlane Toys they call Lord of Darkness. There is even a life-sized casting by sculptor Andy Wright of Artifiex Creations.

The Witches of Eastwick

Jack Nicholson's performance in The Witches of Eastwick is typical of his work, intense, lecherous, and often hysterical. His version of Satan leaves nothing to the imagination, as he uses his powers to cause harm to those who oppose him, and grants the wishes of those who serve. The Devil in this movie has three different women, and as the story unfolds, he exploits their weaknesses, and transforms them into perfect versions of themselves – only to try to kill them. The old expression, Hell hath no fury like a woman scorned certainly applies here!

I highly recommend this movie as it was one of Hollywood's earliest "human" depictions of Lucifer.

The Devil's Advocate

Based on a book by Andrew Neiderman, the film centers on defense attorney Kevin Lomax who has never lost a case. This is my all time favorite film in my collection of Satan. In it we see Keneau Reeves (Kevin) invited to New York to work for a big law firm ruled by senior board member John Milton, masterfully played by Al Pacino. Kevin is showered with wealth and his ego is stoked at every turn. John Milton's fiery speech questions the very notion of righteousness in the post-modern world. Where Milton professes Lucifer lamenting his plight, Pacino's depiction has the Devil still angry and full of fire, saying, "It's the goof of all time.

Look but don't touch. Touch, but don't taste. Taste, don't swallow. Ahaha. And while you're jumpin' from one foot to the next, what is he doing? He's laughin' His sick, f------ ass off! He's a tight-ass! He's a SADIST! He's an absentee landlord! Worship that? NEVER!"

Kevin's dilemma reflects that modern man lives in a culture dominated by making money and balancing his attention on his wife, all in hopes of giving them a better life. In his pursuit to do so, he loses her. This story also touches on the subject of free will, as Milton says one of my favorite lines, "It's like butterfly wings: once touched, they never get off the ground. No, I only set the stage. You pull your own strings."

While assessing the power and actions of the Devil, at least in comparison to other classic tales of Old Scratch, as head of a corporation, Milton was constantly surrounded by minions. An example from the film is perfect to clarify his reasoning:

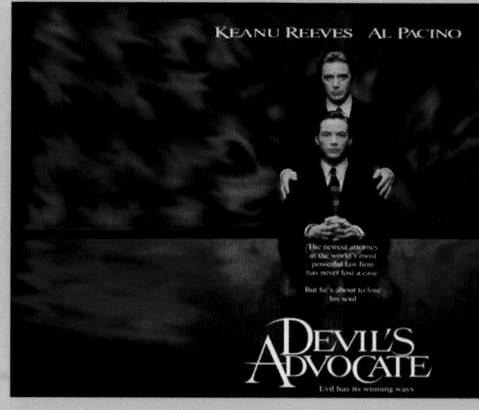

The Devil's Advocate, authors collection.

Kevin Lomax: *Why the law? Cut the shit, Dad! Why the lawyers? Why the law?*

John Milton: *Because the law, my boy, puts us into everything. It's the ultimate backstage pass. It's the new priesthood, baby. Did you know there are more students in law school than lawyers walking the Earth?*

The image of the most recent Devil was that of tempter with power to give one all they wish and is seemingly omniscient, omnipresent, voyeuristic, and sadistic, as the New Testament portrays God, hence Satan is a mirror of his maker. Unlike previous fictional Devils, the image of John Milton was one of triumph.

The image of the Devil as represented in 1926, 1941, and 1997 changed over time. In 1926, the common version of the Devil was with horns and a tail. *The Devil and Daniel Webster* Mr. Scratch appeared as a human with slanted eyebrows and an oblong face. In *The Devil's Advocate*, John Milton did not have any stereotypical physical characterizations that are associated with popular-culture version of the Devil.

Modern Imagery of the Devil

The Devil appears frequently as a character in works of literature and popular culture. Others have portrayed a human character's struggles with Satan in memorable Hollywood performances, such as *Bedazzled* (1967, remade 2000) and *Oh, God! You Devil* (1984). In *Angel on My Shoulder* (1946), the Devil uses the human desire for revenge to his own ends. Neil Gaiman portrays Lucifer in a similar fashion when referenced, such as in his comic series *The Sandman* that formed the basis for the branch-off series, *Lucifer*, which portrays him as an anti-hero after he retires from his position in Hell. Jack Black's Tenacious D summons the Devil in "The Pick of Destiny." Type O Negative's song, "Hallows Eve" is about a man selling his soul to Satan in order to bring his lover back to life on Halloween. Satan has been featured as a character on many popular shows including *South Park, Family Guy, Futurama, The Simpsons,* and *Robot Chicken.* The TV series *Star Trek the Next Generation* has a show called "The Devil's Due," from 1991. In Marvel Comics, in the recent *Ghost Rider series*, Johnny Blaze faces a demon who claims to be Lucifer; he is present in the film adaptation with Nicholas Cage as well.

Chapter Four

The Church of Satan

Organized Satanism is essentially a monotheistic religion which consciously recognizes itself as a heretical offshoot of Christianity. The Church of Satan redefines the seven deadly sins of Christianity – greed, pride, envy, anger, gluttony, lust, and sloth – as satanic virtues. It is materialistic and atheistic, where Satan is a symbol of the individual ego rather than a deity to be worshipped.

The Church of Satan

What is Satanism?

People ask me the question at lectures. It is not a church in the simplest of concepts; it has no building nor traditional worship of a deity. Rather, it is a worship of the ego of the individual, first and foremost. "To the Satanist, he is his own God. Satan is a symbol of Man living as his prideful, carnal nature dictates... Satan is not a conscious entity to be worshipped, rather it is a name for the reservoir of power inside each human to be tapped at will," says the current High Priest of the Church of Satan, Peter H. Gilmore in his book, *The Satanic Scriptures*. Peter H. Gilmore is the High Priest of the Church of Satan. In 2005, Gilmore provided a new introduction to LaVey's *The Satanic Bible*, and his essay on Satanism was published in the *Encyclopedia of Religion and Nature*.

Magister Matt Paradise, the media expert from the Church of Satan and author of *Bearing the Devils Mark* says:

IN SATANISM, SATAN IS AN ARCHETYPE, A REPRESENTATION OF CERTAIN QUALITIES THAT THE SATANIST EMBODIES INCLUDING RATIONAL SELF-INTEREST, AVOIDANCE OF OPPRESSIVE MENTALITIES, THE QUESTIONING OF ALL, AND PERSEVERANCE TOWARDS SUCCESS AND HUMAN POTENTIAL.

Captain Satan. *Courtesy Warlock Draconis of* The Devils Diary *magazine archives.*

Anton Szandor LaVey

In the 1960s, Anton LaVey became the most recognized Satanist in history with *The Satanic Bible;* and in April 1966, *Walpurgisnacht,* The High Priest Anton LaVey, shaved his head in the tradition of Ancient executioners and announced the formation of The Church Of Satan. He had seen the need for a church that would recapture man's body and his carnal desires as objects of celebration. "Since worship of fleshly things produces pleasure," he said, "there would then be a temple of glorious indulgence . . ."

High Priest Anton LaVey.
Courtesy of the Church of Satan.

Satanists are explicit atheists, and proud of it, much like the Humanists. The Church of Satan is founded with concepts of Nietzsche, Ayn Rand, and thinkers like Thomas Paine. "My brand of Satanism," Anton LaVey said, "is the ultimate conscious alternative to herd mentality and institutionalized thought. It is a studied and contrived set of principles and exercises designed to liberate individuals from a contagion of mindlessness that destroys innovation. I have termed my thought 'Satanism' because it is most stimulating under that name. Self-discipline and motivation are affected more easily under stimulating conditions. Satanism means *the opposition* and epitomizes all symbols of nonconformity. Satanism calls forth the strong ability to turn a liability into an advantage, to turn alienation into exclusivity. In other words, the reason it's called Satanism is because it's fun, it's accurate, and it's productive."

In the first year of its foundation, Anton LaVey and the Church of Satan attracted considerable media attention by publicly performing a Satanic marriage of Judith Case and radical journalist John Raymond. The ceremony was photographed by Joe Rosenthal, who took the famous photograph "Raising the Flag on Iwo Jima" during World War II. Another event was the public funeral of Church of Satan member and Naval Officer Edward Olson, at the request of his wife.

Order Of The Trapezoid

Sometime in the 1950s, High Priest Anton LaVey formed a group called the Order of the Trapezoid, which later evolved into the governing body of the Church of Satan. "The Council of Nine, following the dictates of the Nine Unknown, was established throughout the world," says Blanche Barton, Magistra and biographer of the late Church of Satan founder. She went on to say, "Many significant writers have obliquely referred to this mysterious cabal—Shakespeare, John Dryden, Talbot Mundy, Richard Johnson—an archetypal formation which is reflected in the nine members appointed to sit in positions of absolute authority on the United States Supreme Court. The new Age of Fire had been inaugurated, and though the ceremony on Walpurgisnacht, 1966, was a highly personal, private one, LaVey would soon feel the tremors it was to produce. "We blended a formula of nine parts social respectability to one part outrage," Anton LaVey once said. "We established a Church of Satan—something that would smash all concepts of what a 'church' was supposed to be. This was a temple of indulgence to openly defy the temples of abstinence that had been built up until then. We didn't want it to be an unforgiving, unwelcoming place, but a place where you could go to have fun." And thus was initiated two revolutions which have carried over into today: 1) the integration of magic and logic, and 2) a religion based on self-indulgence, carnality (here and now instead of there and then), and pleasure instead of self-denial. Other ego-affirming drew from the ground-breaking attitudes and techniques of the Church of Satan.

"The trapezoid has long been regarded by occultists as the most satanic of shapes, especially adapted to enhance demonic manifestation. Indeed, the middle order of the Satanic brotherhood is called The Order of the Trapezoid," Anton LaVey says as he refers to an occult principle known as the *Law of the Trapezoid*. Anton LaVey says architecture can have an evil, spiritual atmosphere, and his writings tell of geometric angles and spaces." The ancient Atecz, The Egyptians, and Freemasons all used atmosphere to harness and amplify the power of the mind through physical constructs, and Satanism ritual is designed to make the practitioner shake emotional hang-ups, trading fears for ego in order to push to greatest excellence in the outside world.

The Church of Satan was mentioned in many books and was the subject of major magazine and newspaper articles during the 1960s and 1970s. In the 1980s, voices including

Christians, therapists specializing in recovered memories, and the media renewed concerns of criminal conspiracies relating to the Church of Satan. High ranking members of the Church of Satan, such as Magus Peter H. Gilmore, his wife and Priestess Peggy Nadramia, Boyd Rice, publisher Adam Parfrey, Diabolos Rex, and musician King Diamond, were active in media appearances to challenge absurd allegations of criminal activity. (More on this in later chapters on The Satanic Panic.)

In the 1980s and 1990s, the Church of Satan and its members were very active in producing movies, music, films, and magazines devoted to Satanism. Of course, Adam Parfrey's Feral House Publishing, put out *The Satanic Rituals*, *The Satanic Witch*, and during this time, the release of the documentary *Speak of the Devil: The Canon of Anton LaVey*. The Church of Satan and Anton LaVey were also the subject of numerous magazine and news articles.

The position as head of the Church of Satan passed on to Blanche Barton after Anton Szandor LaVey's death. Magistra Barton remains involved in the Church; however, in 2001, she ceded her position to long-time members Peter H. Gilmore and Peggy Nadramia, the current High Priest and High Priestess. As well, the Central Office of the Church of Satan has also moved from San Francisco to New York City's Hell's Kitchen neighborhood, where the couple resides.

The Satanic Bible

High Priest Anton LaVey's greatest known title to this day is his *Satanic Bible*, which has never gone out of print, and having sold hundreds of thousands of copies all over the world in more than half a dozen languages, is the cornerstone of modern Satanism. I will cover the majority of the most important key points, but strongly encourage people to buy a copy for in depth study on their own. Satanism, after all is for the intellectual!

The Satanic Statements

The Nine Satanic Statements are to outline what Satan, within the Church of Satan, symbolizes, perhaps inspired by *Atlas Shrugged*, written by philosopher Ayn Rand.

   † Satan represents indulgence instead of abstinence!
   † Satan represents vital existence instead of spiritual pipe dreams!
   † Satan represents undefiled wisdom instead of hypocritical self-deceit!

- † Satan represents kindness to those who deserve it instead of love wasted on ingrates!
- † Satan represents vengeance instead of turning the other cheek!
- † Satan represents responsibility to the responsible instead of concern for psychic vampires!
- † Satan represents man as just another animal, sometimes better, more often worse than those that walk on all-fours, who, because of his "divine spiritual and intellectual development," has become the most vicious animal of all!
- † Satan represents all of the so-called sins, as they all lead to physical, mental, or emotional gratification!
- † Satan has been the best friend the Church has ever had, as he has kept it in business all these years!

Largely inspired by Nietzsche and similar thinkers, the Church of Satan holds their values in opposition to Judeo-Christianity – their version of sin are the 'sins' that held man back from realizing his fullest potential. They are:

Satanic Sins

1. Stupidity
2. Pretentiousness
3. Solipsism
4. Self-deceit
5. Herd Conformity
6. Lack of Perspective
7. Forgetfulness of Past Orthodoxies
8. Counterproductive Pride
9. Lack of Aesthetics

Eleven Rules of the Earth

Basically, the rules of the Earth are no-brainer, common sense approaches to life by realistic human beings.

- † Do not give opinions or advice unless you are asked.
- † Do not tell your troubles to others unless you are sure they want to hear them.
- † When in another's lair, show him respect or else do not go there.

† If a guest in your lair annoys you, treat him cruelly and without mercy.

† Do not make sexual advances unless you are given the mating signal.

† Do not take that which does not belong to you unless it is a burden to the other person and he cries out to be relieved.

† Acknowledge the power of magic if you have employed it successfully to obtain your desires. If you deny the power of magic after having called upon it with success, you will lose all you have obtained.

† Do not complain about anything to which you need not subject yourself.

† Do not harm little children.

† Do not kill non-human animals unless you are attacked or for your food.

† When walking in open territory, bother no one. If someone bothers you, ask him to stop. If he does not stop, destroy him.

Membership in the Church of Satan

According to the official Church of Satan website, there are two types of members: Registered Members and Active Members. Registered Members are simply people who have been inducted as members of the Church, and there are no requirements to achieve this position. To be deemed an Active Member, a person has to be involved with the Church and local members. Active Membership is divided into five Degrees, beginning with First Degree, simply known as Satanist or member, The Second Degree is titled Warlock, or for the female they are called Witch, for the Third Degree – Priest or Priestess, Fourth Degree they are called Magister o Magistra, Fifth Degree – Magus/Maga. Active Members begin at the First Degree. One must apply and be approved for an Active Membership, higher Degrees one cannot apply for, and the requirements for each degree are not open to the public. Promotion to a higher degree is by invitation only. Members of the Third through Fifth degrees constitute the Priesthood and may be addressed as "Reverend." Officially, The Church of Satan does not recognize any other organizations as holding legitimate claim to Satanism and its practice, though it does recognize that one need not be a member of the Church of Satan to be a Satanist.

High Priest Gilmore at the 06/06/2006 666 Black Mass Ritual in San Francisco.

Satan, Magic, and Ritual in Satanism

Satanism has rituals, and imagery of stereotypical skulls, somber artifacts, candles, and dark drapery. The High Mass is more symbolic still, as more items for the psychodrama, such as gongs and mood music to bring out feelings. Usually, a nude woman is used as an alter to pay respect to the bringer of life (as well as sexuality for Satanist prize man's carnal nature the males are hooded, usually masked and robed to freely express emotions during chants, to not be afraid to release feelings around others participants.

Satanists do not believe that Satan is a god; rather, the function of God is performed and satisfied by the Satanist him/herself. That is, the needs of worship, ritual, and religious/spiritual focus are directed, effectively, inwards towards the Satanist, as opposed to outwards towards a God. The Church of Satan's founder, LaVey, proposes instead, that if all gods are creations of humans, worship of an external deity is worship of its creator by proxy. He suggests, then, that the rational Satanists should instead internalize their gods and therefore worship themselves; hence the Satanic maxim, "I am my own god." In the article *Satanism: The Feared Religion*, High Priest Peter Gilmore explains, "Satanists do not believe in the supernatural, in neither God nor the Devil. To the Satanist, he is his own God. Satan is a symbol of Man living as his prideful, carnal nature dictates. The reality behind Satan is simply the dark evolutionary force of entropy that permeates all of nature and provides the drive for survival and propagation inherent in all living things. Satan is

Satanic Ritual, authors chamber.

not a conscious entity to be worshipped, rather a reservoir of power inside each human to be tapped at will. Thus, any concept of sacrifice is rejected as a Christian concept, for in Satanism, there's no deity to which one can sacrifice."

Taking up the archetype and symbolists view, Satan as a mental/mythic archetype, an anthropomorphic being that is completely fictional: He does not exist as such. However, humanity can identify with him, respect him, and admire him, even as a fictional character or mythic figure as Lucifer

◆◆◆◆

embodies a lot of what Satanists consider important and good qualities, like pride, independence, free-will, intelligence, knowledge, truthfulness, and ambition. For Satanists, Lucifer is a historical and literary archetype. Satanists claim to be adversaries of mainstream behavior which they define as Nietzsche like herd conformity, and belief in Christianity's ideology is stifling to individuality, creativity, and progress.

Magic, as practiced in Satanism, defined in The Book of Belial of *The Satanic Bible*, is "the change in situations or events in accordance with one's will, which would [sic], using normally accepted methods, be unchangeable." This definition incorporates two broadly distinguished kinds of Magic: *Lesser* (manipulative and situational) and *Greater* (ritual and ceremonial). One has to do with knowing people and how to work with them or manipulate situations to one's will, or the use of dress, body language, and proper grooming to attract a mate, as detailed in *The Satanic Witch*. The book was written in correlation to what women desired and could accomplish, as Anton LaVey believed that women could more fully apply his concepts, although the book can be adjusted by males also.

Some Satanists practice their religion free of ritual. They simply follow a lifestyle involving the Satanic statements and rules, while avoiding the Satanic sins. Says High Priest Peter H. Gilmore, "… ritual is natural to people, because humans have a conceptual consciousness. Symbols let us hold much more information in conscious focus, more so than just keeping them separately. So symbols are something we function with. It's part of our nature. So using ritual activities that are symbolic and have deep meaning to us is common to our species if you look at our history from cave paintings up to every civilization currently existing." Others do engage in rituals, frequently involving the following concepts, the Lust ritual from *The Satanic Bible* and *The Satanic Rituals* talk about sex magic which can include masturbation. On June 6, 2006, The Church of Satan held the first public ritual Satanic Mass in forty years at the Steve Allen Theater in the Center for Inquiry in Los Angeles. The ritual, based on the rites outlined in *The Satanic Bible* and *The Satanic Rituals*, was conducted by Reverend Bryan Moore and Priestess Heather Saenz.

The Church of Satan

High Priest Peter H. Gilmore

The current leader and administrator of the Church of Satan is High Priest Peter H. Gilmore. As well, he is the author of and *The Satanic Scriptures*, released in 2007 which contain essays ranging from the similarity between fascist aesthetics and Satanism, along with a multitude of insightful Satanic ideals, and the subject of Terrorism, Gay Rights, and so much more. In many times on documentaries and news interviews, High Priest Peter Gilmore explains the similarities of atheism and Satanism, how science and Darwin's theory of evolution adds to how Satanism is a theatrical "nonreligion." He also shares his opinions about recent strategies to popularize atheism, as well as providing contrasts of Satanic ethics with other nonreligious ethical perspectives such as secular humanism and Objectivism.

Back in 1989, he and his wife Magistra Peggy Nadramia began publishing a Satanic journal, *The Black Flame*, a magazine by and for Satanists. He was appointed High Priest of the Church in 2001 by Magistra Blanche Barton. Within the church, he is known as Magus Peter H. Gilmore, High Priest of the Church of Satan. As a representative of the Church of Satan, Gilmore has been interviewed on modern day Satanism, including appearances on The History Channel, BBC, The Sci-Fi Channel, Point of Inquiry, and a plethora of radio shows.

I personally have had the pleasure of corresponding with High Priest Gilmore over the years and interviewed him in my first book, *Embracing the Darkness: Understanding Dark Subcultures*. As always, he was polite to a fault and quite clear in how he felt about the general public's lack of knowledge on Satanism and pseudo Satanists, like the Heavy Metal Devil worshippers of the 1980s and 1990s. He has publicly said,

My real feeling is that anybody who believes in supernatural entities on some level is insane. Whether they believe in The Devil or God, they are abdicating reason. If they really believe they are in communication with some sort of interventionist deity…you know, somebody can be a deist and think that maybe there was some sort of force that launched everything and now has nothing to do with it. That's not anything you can prove. It's also not a matter of faith. It's a matter of making a choice between whether there was something or there wasn't. I think maybe that is the most rational decision. I think science makes it look otherwise, but I don't think somebody like that is *mad*. But anybody who believes in some kind of existence in deity or spirits or anything that intervenes in their life is not somebody I hold in any kind of esteem…. Lunatic and it's Christian. If you want to believe in an existing Devil then you probably believe in an existing God and you're really just a Christian heretic, you're not a Satanist.

As for the non-spiritual Satanist, he explains:

Satanism begins with atheism. We begin with the universe and say, "It's indifferent. There's no God, there's no Devil. No one cares!" So you then have to make a decision that places yourself at the center of your own subjective universe, because of course we can't have any kind of objective contact with everything that exists. That's rather arrogant and delusional, people who try to put things that way. So by making yourself the primary value in your life, you're your own God. By being your own God, you are comfortable about making your own decisions about what to value. What's positive to you, is good. What harms you, is evil. You extend it to things that you cherish and the people that you cherish. So it's actually very easy to see that it's a self-centered philosophy.

But it also requires responsibility, since you are taking on for yourself the complete onus for your personal success or failure. You can't be praying to a God or blaming a Devil, or anyone else, for that matter, for what happens to you. It's on your own head. That's a challenge for most people. Most people tend to really feel that they want some kind of external support, that they are outward looking and might want some sort of supernatural parental figure, or even some sort of existing governmental authority, existing in their life.

High Priest Peter H. Gilmore.
Courtesy of the Church of Satan.

In answer to how the public fears Satanism today, Magus Gilmore in his article *Satanism: The Feared Religion*, he responds with:

ARE THERE TRULY SOME GROUNDS FOR PEOPLE TO FEEL FEAR AT THE EVER GROWING PHENOMENON OF CONTEMPORARY SATANISM? AS A LONG-TIME PRIEST IN THE CHURCH OF SATAN AND MEDIA REPRESENTATIVE, I CAN CANDIDLY SAY, "YES!" HOWEVER, WHAT THE GENERAL POPULACE HAS DECIDED TO FEAR IS A LUDICROUS PORTRAIT THAT HAS BEEN PAINTED IN LURID TECHNICOLOR BY MEDIA HYPESTERS INTENT ON TITILLATION, EVANGELISTS STRUGGLING TO FILL THEIR COFFERS AND KEEP THEIR MISTRESSES IN JEWELRY, AND MOST DISTRESSINGLY, BY A SEGMENT OF THE THERAPEUTIC COMMUNITY WHO HAVE FOUND A GOLD-MINE IN THE TREATMENT OF SO-CALLED RITUAL ABUSE SURVIVORS WHO PROVIDE NO EVIDENCE OF THEIR TALES OF TERROR (REMARKABLY SIMILAR TO STORIES TOLD BY WOMEN LABELED BY FREUD AS HYSTERICS), SAVE FOR THEIR FERVENT BELIEF THAT THEY WERE VICTIMIZED.

I SHALL NOT WASTE TIME IN REFUTING THE ABSURD CLAIM THAT THERE IS AN INTERNATIONAL CONSPIRACY OF GENERATIONAL SATANISTS BENT ON ENSLAVING THE WORLD THROUGH DRUG USE AND SACRIFICE OF BABIES BRED FOR THAT PURPOSE BY EMOTIONALLY UNSTABLE WOMEN. THAT MYTHOLOGY HAS BEEN THOROUGHLY EXPLORED BY OTHER SOURCES (THE FBI'S *NATIONAL CENTER FOR THE ANALYSIS OF VIOLENT CRIME: INVESTIGATOR'S GUIDE TO ALLEGATIONS OF RITUAL CHILD ABUSE*, JANUARY 1992; THE COMMITTEE FOR SCIENTIFIC EXAMINATION OF RELIGION'S REPORT *SATANISM IN AMERICA*, OCTOBER 1989; THE BRITISH GOVERNMENT'S DEPARTMENT OF HEALTH REPORT: *THE EXTENT AND NATURE OF ORGANIZED AND RITUAL ABUSE*, HMSO, 1994). LET US INSTEAD LOOK AT CONTEMPORARY SATANISM FOR WHAT IT REALLY IS: A BRUTAL RELIGION OF ELITISM AND SOCIAL DARWINISM THAT SEEKS TO RE-ESTABLISH THE REIGN OF THE ABLE OVER THE IDIOTIC, OF SWIFT JUSTICE OVER INJUSTICE, AND FOR A WHOLESALE REJECTION OF EGALITARIANISM AS A MYTH THAT HAS CRIPPLED THE ADVANCEMENT OF THE HUMAN SPECIES FOR THE LAST TWO THOUSAND YEARS. IS THAT SOMETHING TO FEAR? IF YOU'RE ONE OF THE MAJORITY OF HUMAN MEDIOCRITIES MERELY EXISTING AS A MEDIA-BESOTTED DRONE, YOU BET IT IS!

Many famous figures have been a part of the Church of Satan, including Kenneth Anger, professional wrestler Balls Mahoney, professional wrestler Sterling James Keenan, journalist Michael Moynihan, Death Metal Lead Guitarist Matthew McRaith, Sammy Davis, Jr., and the artist Coop. The Church of Satan does not publicly release membership information; it is not known how many members belong to the Church.

A lot has been said of what Satanists are in the media, the general public who simply doesn't know better, as well as explanations of what the beliefs of Satanists think like. But Satanism is a religion of action not of faith. The members are highly intelligent, professional, and creative types. I'd like to share with you some insights from some friends and acquaintances to demonstrate a clearer picture of what these individuals actually do. You might be quite surprised how normal they are!

Satanic Scriptures, by High Priest Peter H. Gilmore. *Courtesy of Scapegoat Publishing.*

THE SATANIC SCRIPTURES

Peter H. Gilmore

Magister Frost, the founder of The CosEmporium online store and head administrator of the popular "Letters to the Devil" forum shared his beginnings in the Church of Satan with me in detail. What he had to say was very enlightening for me as one so young to advance as high as he has, proof in showing the organization does not hold people back despite typical barriers found elsewhere. Magister Alexander Frost says,

I BECAME INTERESTED IN SATANISM AFTER READING *THE SATANIC BIBLE* WHEN I WAS BETWEEN THE AGES OF 13 AND 14. THE THING THAT AMAZED ME ABOUT *THE SATANIC BIBLE* WAS THE FACT THAT THE BOOK DID NOT SHOW ME A "PATH" TO SOME FALSE ENLIGHTENMENT BUT IN FACT IT SHOWED ME THE THINGS I ALREADY KNEW. *THE SATANIC BIBLE* RE-ENFORCED MY PERSONAL FEELINGS ABOUT LIFE AND THE WORLD AROUND ME. IT ALSO SHOWED ME THAT THERE WERE OTHERS OUT THERE WHO FELT LIKE I DID, LIKE-MINDED INDIVIDUALS.

I JOINED THE CHURCH OF SATAN AT AGE 16, BECAME AN ACTIVE MEMBER AT AGE 18, WAS INVITED TO THE PRIESTHOOD AT AGE 22, APPOINTED TO MAGISTER AT AGE 30. I WAS FIRST INVITED TO DR. LAVEY'S BLACK HOUSE LOCATED IN SAN FRANCISCO IN 1997 AND I WOULD HAVE TO SAY THAT WAS THE BEST EXPERIENCE OF MY LIFE.

I DEVELOPED THE FIRST SATANIC WEBSITE BACK WHEN THE INTERNET WAS FIRST BORN, WHICH NOW HAS BECOME A SECOND HOME TO A LARGE NUMBER OF SATANISTS AROUND THE WORLD. THE WEBSITE LEAD TO VARIOUS NATIONWIDE RADIO INTERVIEWS ALONG WITH BEING FEATURED ON MANY TELEVISION NETWORKS (TBS, CNN, NBC, CBS, ETC) AND ENDED UP BEING FEATURED IN JUST ABOUT EVERY MAGAZINE PUBLISHED BACK IN THE LATE 1990S. IT HAS EVOLVED OVER THE LAST DECADE INTO A CENTRAL HUB FOR COMMUNICATION AND INFORMATION BASED ON TOPICS THAT INTEREST SATANISTS WHICH CURRENTLY HAS OVER 10,000 REGISTERED USERS.

I ALSO CREATED THE FIRST ONLINE STORE FOR DIRECTLY DEALING IN SATANIC PRODUCTS. THE COS EMPORIUM STARTED OUT AS A ONE PAGE LISTING OF ADDRESSES WHERE YOU COULD ORDER PRODUCTS AND IT GREW INTO A FULLY FLEDGED ONLINE STORE WHERE YOU CAN ORDER JUST ABOUT EVERYTHING A SATANIST'S HEART COULD DESIRE. FUELED BY MY DESIRE TO DEVELOP "SATANIC FRIENDLY" BUSINESSES WHICH CATER TO THOSE OF US WITH A "DARKER" SIDE, I BEGAN OPENING OTHER TYPES OF BUSINESSES. I CREATED A FEW CANDLE/ FRAGRANCE COMPANIES, A WEBSITE HOSTING BUSINESS, A MUSIC/ RECORD PRODUCTION COMPANY (LE'RUE DELASHAY WAS MY FIRST RELEASED ARTIST), AND A FEW OTHER LITTLE VENTURES OVER THE YEARS. I ALSO HAVE A FEW NEW IDEAS FOR COMPANIES I WOULD LIKE TO BUILD IN THE FUTURE, BUT EVERYONE WILL HAVE TO WAIT AND SEE TO FIND OUT WHAT THOSE ARE!

Magister Frost Letters to the Devil.
Courtesy of Magister Frost.

The Art of Storm and Dark Queen Apparel

The wife of tattoo artist and Satanic husband, Storm Anderson was gracious enough to answers a few questions for me as well, and talk about her rock inspired clothing line. She said, "The idea for Dark Queen Apparel originally came about 4 to 5 years ago when my Husband and I were getting ready to attend a concert. I wanted to wear something that would reflect my love for heavy metal. I searched high and low but could not find anything satisfying. I was frustrated at the thought of being able to find t-shirts for just about every band out there for men. I considered that to be quite sexist so I decided to purchase one and take my twelve-plus years of sewing experience and reconstruct it for myself. The compliments started rolling in and Dark Queen Apparel was born!"

This creative couple from Salt Lake City, Utah, has been a host of various events and featured in *Rue Morgue*. I asked Storm what did she attribute to the quick rise to attention and how did she fit in being a full-time business woman as well as a mother of three? Storm replied, "Everyday I manifest wicked works on canvas, horror dolls, and the flesh. Managing *Attatude Tattoo*, running *Art on You*, assisting my Wife, The Dark Queen, with her business, *Dark Queen Apparel*, and raising the two young ladies who still live with us also add to keeping me very busy. When I'm not attending to that aggregation of responsibilities, my Queen and I enjoy carnal indulgences, attending dark events, Metal shows, fine liquors and foods, and meeting unique individuals."

Storm also revealed, "Creating art is truly innate for me. I couldn't fathom not being an Artist. As I was attending school at Idaho State University, I developed *Art on You*. After leaving Pocatello for Salt Lake City and meeting my Queen, I was encouraged to take the name *Art on You* and apply it literally through the Tattoo Industry. Once introduced to the Tattoo World, I was exposed to influences such as Bob Tyrrell and Paul Booth. Knox, my mentor and owner of *Attatude Tattoo*, and Reuben, friend and colleague at *Attatude*, have been nurturing my progress as a Tattoo Artist. Slinging ink has become my primary focus; however, while drawing on the inspirations of Horror literature and films, Heavy Metal music, and other Artists such as HR Giger, Dali, Coop, Eric Pigors, Magister Diabolus Rex, and others, I am constantly evolving my demonic dolls and canvas works. My greatest muse, of course, is my Queen." When asked about whether they'd experienced any backlash in their town due to their imagery, and blatant connection to Satanism, he had a few surprising comments, saying "Living in Salt Lake City, one would assume that the LDS folks shun me and my creations, but Salt Lake is a major metropolitan area and I am one of a throng of like-minded individuals who no longer shock the majority of church-going people. Certainly there are a handful

Dark Queen Renee Anderson.

Storm Anderson, Church of Satan
ART ON YOU STUDIO.

of religious zealots who would condemn my blasphemous works and I greatly appreciate them as it is confirmation that I am following my desired path. Our neighbors have become accustomed to the *Addam's Family* decor they can view through our windows and open doors, as well as the variety of Baphomet and dark-natured flags we wave throughout the year. Further, on 6/6/6 and the days leading up to the dreaded holiday, I was featured on FOX News and in local publications due to me spearheading Salt Lake's *Opening the Gates of Hell* party, and not once was I ostracized for my convictions. In fact, I'm slowly gaining a small following of local fans of my Dark Art."

Witchy Goodness

Back in February of 2008, I went traveling across the country for the grand opening brick and mortar store, FeMaledictions and found some truly fantastic works of original art, meticulously selected books, as well as witchcraft and Satanic goods ritual items, jewelry, and one-of-a-kind collectibles located in beautiful, historic downtown Stoughton, Wisconsin, a mere twenty minutes southeast of Madison. The beautiful Witch, Sara, was delightfully warm and I certainly would enjoy another road trip to visit again.

Other members are models, such as Marilyn Mansfield who has been featured in *Old Nick*, *The Ninth Gate Magazine* and *Penthouse*, as well as a participant in fashion shows. There

FeMaleaddictions grand opening in 2008, author with Witch Sara.

Jason Leach ☯

Artist Warlock Daniel Byrd

Goat rendering, pen and ink by Warlock Daniel Byrd

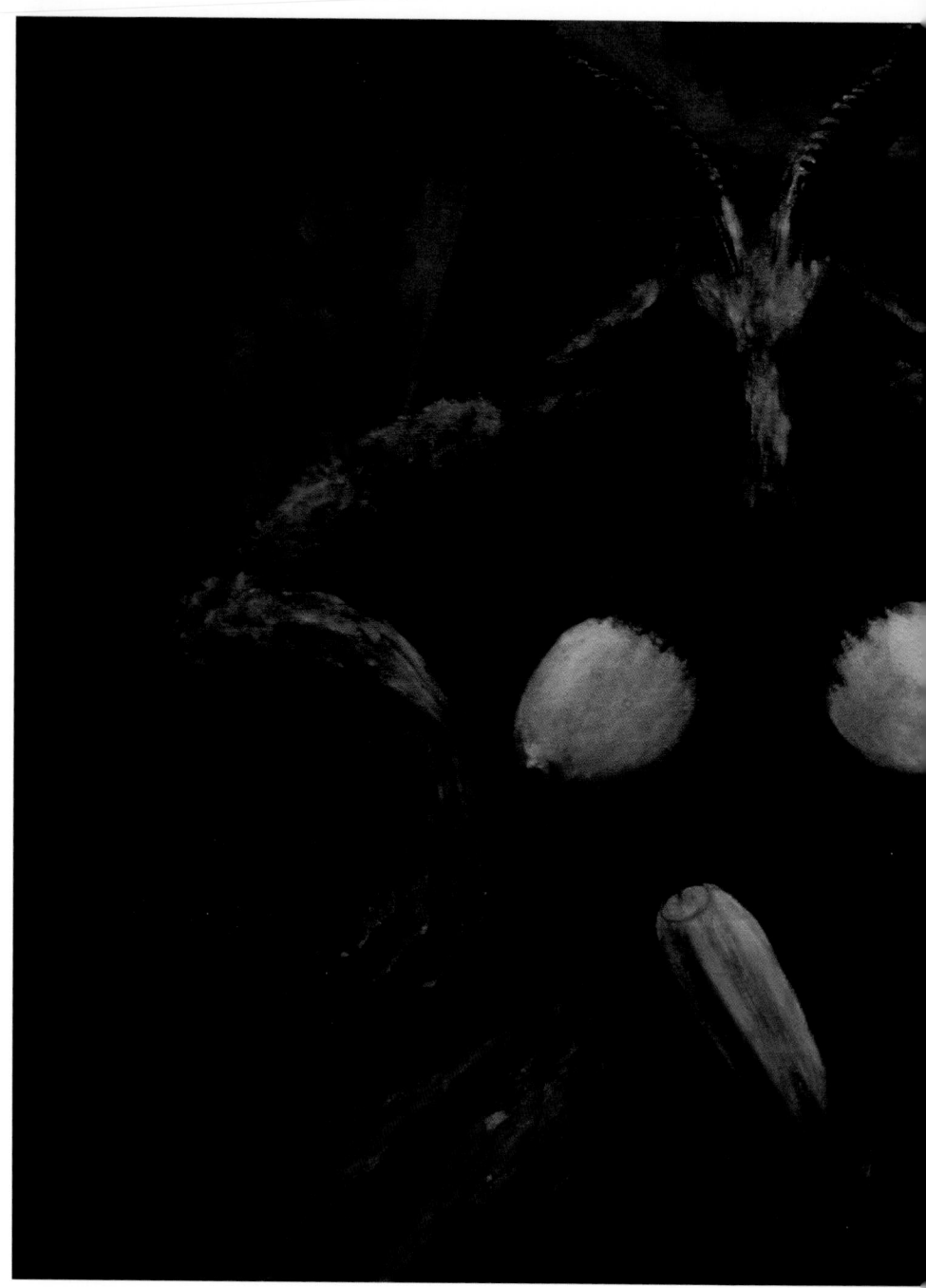

Baphomet depicted by artist Warlock Daniel Byrd

Devil cane, original design by Warlock Corvis
Nocturnum, sculpt and casting by Warlock Jason
Leach, sculptor

The Devil's Studio, the art of Warlock Jason Leach *Elder Eye.*

Squirm, by artist Warlock Jason Leach bronze finish 2010.

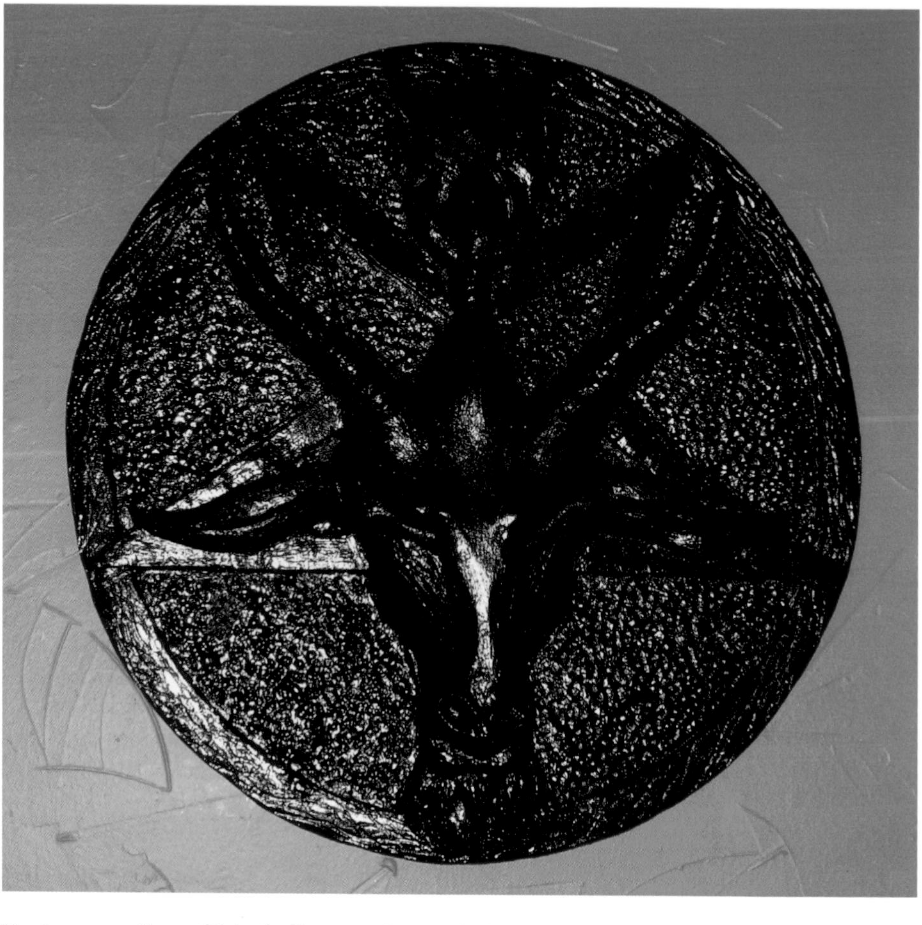

Baphomet wall art, 20-inch diameter, by Warlock Nocturnum, 2009.

Sympathy for the Devil. Courtesy Dark Moon Press.

Teaching the Youth
2005 ce, Acrylic
on Found LDS
Object art by Storm
Anderson, 11 x 14

Storm Anderson's
tattoo art book,
Devil's sketchbook.

Witch Scarlet Norton, publisher of Diabolic Publications.

Diabolic Publications cover. *Courtesy of publisher.*

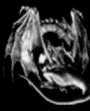

Silk Stockings
Legs of Seduction

Silk Stockings: Legs of Seduction

Diabolic Publications

George Sprague

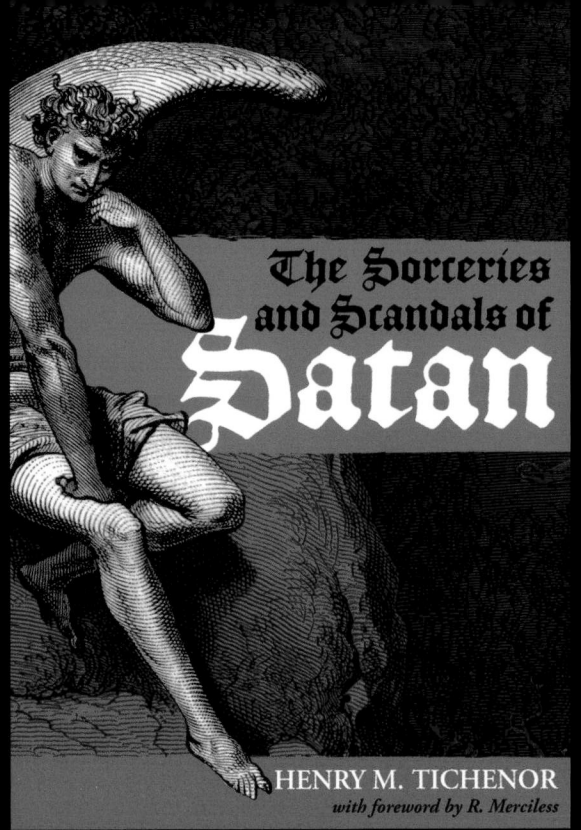

The Sorceries and Scandals of Satan

HENRY M. TICHENOR
with foreword by R. Merciless

Chapter Five

Lucifer's Wayward Children

Scandals of Satan – Underworld. Special thanks to
Kevin I. Slaughter, publisher.

Rock, the Highway to Hell

The Devil has long been associated with secular music. The myth of the virtuoso fiddler who sold his soul to the Devil at the crossroads was translated into American folklore with a long history of Blues players selling their souls for Devilishly good musical abilities. The relationship between metal and Lucifer is often very clear and explicit with many

Ventriloquo di Dio or *Portrait of Lucifer Playing the Violin.*

bands, Black and Death metal bands in particular, labeling themselves as Satanic, but even classic heavy metal seems to have a direct tie to Satan by evangelists. Once upon a time, innocently dancing in a family setting was viewed as sinful by Puritanical extremists. In 1976, David Bowie famously told us that "Rock has always been the Devil's music," in *Rolling Stone* magazine, and added, "I believe rock and roll is dangerous... I feel we're only heralding something even darker than ourselves." (*Rolling Stone*, February 12, 1976). "Christianity as a whole looks at man's carnal wants as major sins when taken to excess when one indulges in the pleasures of the flesh: food, drink, sex, even dance and music. But to real Satanism, over-indulgence in one's 'sin' is merely the Satanic Sin of stupidity, hardly worthy of torment beyond physical discomfort! Sex and Lust influenced by the Devil is pretty much just our carnal, human nature put to song, just as it always has been in bawdy lyrics of old. This isn't a new phenomenon from the 1900s. But the Devil is certainly given his due in rock and roll if not in any other means of expressionism since the Romantic writers of their day."

A book on rock as it pertains to contemporary art and culture, *Sympathy for the Devil: Art and Rock and Roll Since 1967*, examines the inspired relationship between the visual arts and rock-and-roll culture, featuring album cover art and music videos. Its detailed essays describe rock and roll's style, proving their case well, that artists have maintained a strong connection to rock. The majority of those who've adopted the Satanic imagery have done so out of sensationalism and the desire to amass wealth from the notoriety.

Early Minions

As with the early "rock stars" during the Romantic Period, like Lord Byron who used to say he was like the Devil himself, modern rock follows the same pattern in sexuality in presentation and in its words. We see so much androgyny or sexual "confusion," rebellion is naturally attracted to the repressed, the taboo. Foremost among such repressed desires were sexuality, and as rock music had some early obvious examples of mimicry of the sex itself, i.e., Elvis Presley when he infamously, on national television, made obscene gyrations of his pelvis.

Heavy metal surfaced in the '80s and '90s, offering not only repressed sexuality, but also the repressed aggression and blood of bodily violence evident via the mosh pit. The accompanying noise, violence, and pyrotechniques of the concert would have made theologians of day's past imagine they had opened the gates of Hell itself! Gavin Baddely, author of *Lucifer Rising*, did a magnificent study in the ways the Devil has been cited and has influenced rock and roll. I will touch on the key highlights, plus add in a lot of my own research so as not to stay off topic and provide history of side events as Gavin Baddley did, to keep things easier to follow.

The Rolling Stones

Between 1963 and 1964 the *Beatles* and the *Rolling Stones* assaulted Western European and American culture with their lyrics, and millions of fans unheard of prior to this time, swelled amphitheaters everywhere.

"Sympathy for the Devil" is by far the most memorable Rolling Stones' track, and was intended to be more of a commentary on the violence of humanity throughout the ages:

PLEASE ALLOW ME TO INTRODUCE MYSELF
I'M A MAN OF WEALTH AND TASTE
I'VE BEEN AROUND FOR A LONG, LONG YEAR
STOLE MANY A MAN'S SOUL AND FAITH.

Mick Jagger attempting to level the field a bit, during an interview commented once,

WHEN PEOPLE STARTED TAKING US AS DEVIL WORSHIPERS, I THOUGHT IT WAS A REALLY ODD THING, BECAUSE IT WAS ONLY ONE SONG, AFTER ALL. IT WASN'T LIKE IT WAS A WHOLE ALBUM, WITH LOTS OF OCCULT SIGNS ON THE BACK. PEOPLE SEEMED TO EMBRACE THE IMAGE SO READILY; IT HAS CARRIED ALL THE WAY OVER INTO HEAVY METAL BANDS TODAY.

Keith Richards said in 1971 to *Rolling Stone* magazine on the band's image,

> BEFORE, WE WERE JUST INNOCENT KIDS OUT FOR A GOOD TIME, THEY'RE SAYING, "THEY'RE EVIL, THEY'RE EVIL." OH, I'M EVIL, REALLY? SO THAT MAKES YOU START THINKING ABOUT EVIL… WHAT IS EVIL? HALF OF IT, I DON'T KNOW HOW MUCH PEOPLE THINK OF MICK AS THE DEVIL OR AS JUST A GOOD ROCK PERFORMER OR WHAT? THERE ARE BLACK MAGICIANS WHO THINK WE ARE ACTING AS UNKNOWN AGENTS OF LUCIFER AND OTHERS WHO THINK WE ARE LUCIFER. EVERYBODY'S LUCIFER.

"Sympathy For The Devil" was on the release of *Interview With The Vampire* when Guns n' Roses played the song for the film's soundtrack, and in 2004, it made number thirty-four on *Rolling Stone's* 500 Greatest Songs of All Time.

The Devil and Occultism in Rock

The Beatles

Beatle John Lennon made a statement to the international press back in 1966:

> CHRISTIANITY WILL GO. IT WILL GO. IT WILL VANISH AND SHRINK. I NEEDN'T ARGUE ABOUT THAT. I'M RIGHT AND I WILL BE PROVED RIGHT. WE ARE MORE POPULAR THAN JESUS NOW.

And he also stated once that:

> THE WHOLE BEATLE IDEA WAS TO DO WHAT YOU WANT, RIGHT? TO TAKE YOUR OWN RESPONSIBILITY, DO WHAT YOU WANT, AND TRY NOT TO HARM OTHER PEOPLE, RIGHT? DO WHAT THOU WILST, AS LONG AS IT DOESN'T HURT SOMEBODY. . .
>
> *THE PLAYBOY INTERVIEWS*
> JOHN LENNON AND YOKO ONO

One of Crowley's most devout disciples was Led Zeppelin guitarist, Jimmy Page, who even bought "The Beasts" home, located on Lock Ness – rumor has it Crowley was buried inside a dark chamber in Boleskine. Page had inscribed Crowley's most famous "Do what thou wilt shalt be the whole of the

The complete collection of

Dark Moon Press

law" in the vinyl on Zeppelin's Third album, *Led Zeppelin III,* and admitted he performed Crowley rituals during some of their concerts. Ozzy Osbourne, who jokingly called himself through his career "the prince of Darkness," called Crowley a "phenomenon of his time," (*Circus,* August, 26, 1980) and recorded a song of tribute to Crowley in *Mr. Crowley:*

> *. . . You fooled all the people with magic*
> *You waited on Satan's call . . .*
> *Mr. Crowley, won't you ride my white horse...*

The complete collection of Aliester Crowley. Courtesy Dark Moon Press.

The Eagles' manager, Larry Salter, admitted in the *Waco Tribune-Herald* (February 28, 1982), that the Eagles were involved with the Church of Satan, and Frank Zappa proudly boasted, "I'm the Devil's advocate. We have our own worshippers who are called groupies. Girls will give their bodies to musicians as you would give a sacrifice to a god." (Peters Brothers, *What About Christian Rock,* p. 17.) Carlos Santana admits to being controlled by demons, and having NO concern for morality or God:

> THE ENERGY OF DEVILS AND ANGELS IS THE SAME ENERGY; IT'S HOW YOU USE IT. IT'S FUEL. THERE IS A SAYING: IF YOU SCARE ALL YOUR DEVILS AWAY, THE ANGELS WILL GO AWAY WITH THEM. YOU KNOW, THE HALO AND THE HORNS ARE THE SAME THING. I MEAN IT'S OKAY TO BE SPIRITUALLY HORNY – THAT'S WHAT CREATIVE GENIUS IS ALL ABOUT. GENIUSES DON'T HAVE TIME TO THINK ABOUT HOW IT'S GOING TO BE RECEIVED... THEY DON'T HAVE TIME TO THINK WHETHER PEOPLE LIKE IT OR NOT, IS IT MORALLY RIGHT, WILL GOD LIKE IT?
>
> ~ Carlos Santana
> *Rolling Stone,* March 16, 2000

During the 1970s, *Hotel California* by the Eagles was rumored to have on the inside of the album cover, looking down on the festivities, a blurred image of Anton LaVey, the founder of the Church of Satan and author of *The Satanic Bible.* The Eagles manager, Larry Salter, admitted in the *Waco Tribune-Herald,* (February 28, 1982) that the Eagles were involved with the Church of Satan, but little evidence has been brought forth that it was anything but publicity to sell records.

Overt Satanism and occultism outside of anything short of "satanic death metal" (which is more like Luciferiansism) fell by the wayside unless it was a small mention or symbol thrown in for nostalgia or effect. Tipper Gore back in 1987, author of *Raising PG Kids in an X-Rated Society*, commented on satanic heavy metal bands:

> THIS CHILDHOOD FASCINATION WITH THE OCCULT HAS LED TO ONE OF THE MOST SICKENING MARKETING GIMMICKS IN HISTORY.

Bands like Motley Crue's *(Shout at the Devil)* did so in tongue-in-cheek and were not even occultists like a few of the 1960s band members. Occultism was simply another sign of rebellion against the mainstream. As time continued and less shocked the public at large, one man stepped forward to be the Devil's advocate to give one last shock to rock in the name of all that is blasphemous, Marilyn Manson.

Marilyn Manson
Anti-Christ Super Star

One of the more blatant Satanic performers was Marilyn Manson. Manson was originally a music journalist before he got into music. He moved to Florida when he was 18 and began to write stories and poems. He tried to get his poems and stories published by various magazines, and it was while covering *Nine Inch Nails* for his magazine that Brian Warner was given an opportunity to meet Trent Reznor. Reznor sponsored the soon-to-be infamous band – and eventually produced their first three albums. Manson later changed his name to Marilyn Manson as he liked to shock people by pairing the two opposites – beauty meets Marilyn Monroe and glorifying Charles Manson. It was when he was an Antichrist Superstar that he began burning Bibles in his concerts saying, "I think every time people listen to this new album maybe God will be destroyed in their heads." Manson made a statement posted on his Web site:

> I'VE ALWAYS HAD A DESIRE TO BE PROVOCATIVE AND TO MAKE PEOPLE THINK, BUT IT WOULDN'T BE ANY CHALLENGE FOR ME JUST TO BE SHOCKING. THAT IS WHERE IT BEGINS FOR ME, NOT WHERE IT STOPS. AND I COULD BE MUCH MORE SHOCKING. I THINK I'VE ADOPTED A SENSE OF SUBTLETY. I DON'T SIT AROUND WONDERING HOW I CAN MAKE MYSELF EVEN STRANGER TO THE WORLD. I'VE SIMPLY EVOLVED INTO THE MONSTER I CREATED, AND I'M QUITE HAPPY WITH IT.

Manson admits his childhood longing for Satan, saying, "My mom used to tell me when I was a kid, 'If you curse at nighttime, the Devil's going to come to you when you're sleeping.' I used to get excited because I really wanted it to happen . . . I wanted it. I wanted it more than anything." (*Rolling Stone*, January, 23, 1997.) While on tour, the shock-rocker received an invitation to meet with Anton LaVey at his home. At the end of the visit, Manson was made a priest in the Church of Satan; he poses for a photo with LaVey in front of a large Baphomet. A photo is later reprinted in Manson's 1998 autobiography *The Long Hard Road Out of Hell*; the *New York Times* best seller is dedicated to the memory of Anton LaVey. The year 1998 also saw the publication of a posthumous LaVey essay collection, *Satan Speaks!* with an introduction by Marilyn Manson. His own favorite authors, other than Anton LaVey, were Frederick Nietzsche, Aleister Crowley, and Charles Darwin. Although he made news as a member of the Priesthood of The Church of Satan, the leader of the church says,

HE'S A MEMBER WHO HAS BEEN GIVEN AN HONORARY PRIESTHOOD. WHEN ASKED ABOUT WHAT SATANISM IS, HE CAN BE VERY ARTICULATE IN EXPLAINING IT. BUT HIS OWN MUSIC IS HIS OWN ART. HIS STAGE SHOWS ARE HIS OWN, AND THEY DON'T REALLY EXEMPLIFY SATANISM IN PARTICULAR.... IF ASKED ABOUT OUR PHILOSOPHIES, HE CAN EXPLAIN IT. THE INTERESTING THING IS WHEN HIS FIRST ALBUM CAME OUT, THE TWO OF US MET ON A PANEL THAT WE WERE DOING ABOUT RACISM IN MUSIC THAT WAS BEING SPONSORED BY *SECONDS MAGAZINE*. NOBODY KNEW WHO BRIAN WARNER WAS AT THAT POINT, AND HE CAME UP TO ME AND GAVE ME A CD AND HE WAS ALL IN COSTUME. BUT HE SAID, 'I HEARD ABOUT YOU AND I WANTED TO MEET YOU,' SO WE MOVED ASIDE AND TALKED FOR A LITTLE WHILE AND I LEARNED HE REALLY DID UNDERSTAND SATANISM. I TOLD ANTON LAVEY THAT THIS GUY WAS PRETTY SMART AND THIS GIMMICK IS GOING TO DO WELL; IT'S CLEVER. HE'S USING THIS SERIAL KILLER AND HOLLYWOOD STAR COMBINATION, AND HE'S A SMART GUY AND CREATING HIS OWN PERSONA THAT IS PROBABLY GOING TO BE SUCCESSFUL. IT TOOK OFF IMMEDIATELY, AND WHEN MARILYN MANSON WAS OUT ON TOUR IN CALIFORNIA, HE ASKED IF HE COULD MEET ANTON LAVEY AND HE WAS IMPRESSED. HE IS A REALLY SWEET AND SINCERE GUY, WHICH HAS NOTHING TO DO WITH WHAT ALL OF THE WORLD SEES IN JUST HIS ACT AND HIS ART.

When Marilyn Manson performed live on the MTV European Video Music Awards in Dublin, Ireland, for an estimated one billion viewers, he said,

IT WAS RATHER IRONIC THAT TEENAGE GIRLS WITH BREAST IMPLANTS AND RAPPERS WITH VIOLENT AND MISOGYNISTIC LYRICS SPENT THE WHOLE NIGHT THANKING JESUS CHRIST OF ALL PEOPLE. IT IS CLEARLY BY UNCHRISTIAN MEANS THAT THESE ALLEGED "FRIENDS OF GOD" HAVE MADE THEIR MILLIONS SO I CHOSE A MORE HONEST WAY TO SAY THANKS.

In *USA Today*, November 21, 2000, Manson reflected on the Devil directly and how he himself is involved to the general public at large, as he said,

There's an old saying - The Devil is the church's best friend. If Satan wasn't around, churches would go out of business. The same goes for conservatives or Christians, or whoever they might be. They need art because art is evil; art challenges beliefs. Because I'm a vocal spokesperson for that kind of activity, I am the Devil to them.

Black Metal Takes the Stage

Death Metal and/or Black Metal are probably the most readily stereotyped and most-often criticized forms of music, and are most often affected with a negative public image. Matthew, the founder and lead-singer of the death-metal band, Shroud, helps to clear up some gray areas and misconceptions about this genre of music, saying,

> A lot of Death Metal tends to focus on political issues, even a horror movie put to music, to some extent. Black Metal is more oriented to left Hand Path magic or Satanic. I would just call us more LHP (Left Hand Path), sort of a follower of the dark side, an emphasis on Dark Gods.

And having been at Dark Horizon records, which operates from my hometown supplying CDs across the globe to stores and online customers, it is a fairly well-known part of the Black and Death Metal music industry. Its owner, Lord Typhus, has been featured in *Pit Magazine* and is also the lead singer in the band TYPHUS. Its owner, Lord Typhus, has been featured in *Pit Magazine* and is also the lead singer in TYPHUS. Both Lord Typhus and his bassist, Evil Priest, were very obliging when approached for an interview. One of the first questions that came to my mind as I researched was, as a distributor of Black and Death Metal in America and abroad, would there be any validity to the claim that these groups like this are musical terrorists? Typhus replied,

> Well, there is that percentage that have taken action like Emperor, Dissection, and others that have actually murdered people for fame. They were the martyrs for a cause. Now it has exploded into a marketable thing…. There is a small fraction of extremists that play the music, that live it, and kind of step to the next level, which is actually breaking the law. That handful of individuals made it a fashionable, marketable thing by getting all of us attention. …A vehicle for notoriety. It's not the route I would go; trading your freedom in exchange for a reputation of burning a church down is pretty stupid…. You will always have that fringe section that use music as an excuse to break the law. Normal, intelligent people who listen to this will not…. We offer artistic expression. I play in two bands; I think it is a form of aggressive art form, of expression that is not for everyone. I think with the explosion of bands coming out all over the world, finally, like Dimmu Borgir, active Satanist who are actively in the spotlight who are looked upon by movie producers, TV producers. We want to be recognized as legitimate artists who have a message. We convey a thought. Satanic artists spread their political messages, hip hop culture spreads theirs, and it's all the same.

Album artwork for Dimmu Borgir's *In Sorte Diaboli* album features a classic depiction of the Devil. Ancient pattern of pre Christian pagan influences on a genre of music, as is anti-Christianity and horror, are a bigger part of this scene, so too is the fascination with evil itself, revealing an interest in delving into dark. They embrace various empowering philosophies of individualism, a selfish rationality, of the Devil. Rock music, Heavy Metal and even rock music in general are representative in the cultural consciousness of the over-indulgence and repression of who we are. Perhaps, as I suspect, it is a counter swing of the scales to lash out at the centuries of oppressive dogma rebelling against the Church. They were rebelling against intolerance, of those of whom they see as the enemy. Are there true Satanic bands you might ask? The answer is yes. The Quintessentials, a band out of Oregon via Hawaii, founded by Warlock Les Hernandez. has been known to tour with the likes of Bad Religion, Blink 182, and L.A. Guns, and have had their album covers featured on the History Channel documentary *Hell: the Devil's Domain*. The charismatic musician was kind enough to offer me not only images for this book, but his personal thoughts on Satan and what it means to him personally.

ASK MOST SUPPOSEDLY SERIOUS "SATANIC" BANDS IN THE METAL GENRE WHAT SATANISM REPRESENTS TO THEM AND YOU'RE MORE THAN LIKELY TO HEAR THE MANTRA "FREEDOM" REPEATED WITHOUT MUCH ELABORATION AS TO EXACTLY WHAT THAT MEANS. TO ME THAT'S A COP-OUT. SURE, SATAN REPRESENTS FREEDOM, BUT FROM WHAT?

SATAN IS, IN MY ARTISTIC OR MUSICAL USE, BOTH THE DEAMON OR MUSE WHICH INSPIRES AND THE MANIFESTATION OR REALIZATION THAT RESULTS FROM THAT INSPIRATION. IN OTHER WORDS, SATAN CREATES THE SPIRIT OF INNOVATION AND INSPIRATION THAT CAUSES ME TO ACTION – TO MAKE MUSIC. WHEN THAT MUSIC OR ART IS MADE REAL, IT IS SATANIC IN THAT IT, TOO, INSPIRES OTHERS. SURE, SATAN REPRESENTS REBELLION FROM HERD MENTALITY, BUT SATAN ALSO PUSHES THE INDIVIDUAL TO GREATER HEIGHTS OF PERSONAL ACCOMPLISHMENT. THAT NUDGE OR INFERNAL PRODDING TO CREATE MAKES ONE A CREATOR, AND WE ALL KNOW THAT TO CREATE IS TO "PLAY GOD." SO, THROUGH SATAN, THE ARTIST (WHATEVER ART IS HIS MEDIUM) IS BROUGHT TO GODHOOD.

OF COURSE, IT SHOULD BE NOTED THAT SATAN IS ONE'S INNER-MOST SELF TO BEGIN WITH AND NOT SOME SORT OF EXTERNAL FATHER-FIGURE OR LITERAL "SPIRITUAL" ENTITY. MAINSTREAM RELIGIONISTS WOULD HAVE YOU BELIEVE THAT SATAN WISHES TO CORRUPT VIA ART AND THE MEDIA. THE TRUTH IS THAT MAINSTREAM INDOCTRINATION IS THE CORRUPTER. MAN IS BORN A PURE ANIMAL – INNOCENCE. MAINSTREAM RELIGION TEACHES HIM THAT THIS INNOCENCE AND NATURAL INSTINCT IS EVIL. SATAN IS THE METAPHORICAL REPRESENTATION OF THAT PURITY WE ALL WERE BEFORE CORRUPTION. THE MEDIA IS INDEED A TOOL USED FOR CORRUPTION, BUT CORRUPTION BY UNNATURAL "GOD" RELIGIONS, NOT BY SATANISM. IF ANY FORM OF DEVIL WORSHIP EXISTS IN THE MEDIA, IT WAS CREATED BY THOSE GOD ADORERS TO SCARE PEOPLE BACK INTO CHURCH – AND SIMPLY BACKFIRED. THEY SHOULDN'T MISTAKE THEIR CREATION FOR SATANISM.

THAT BEING SAID, DO I GLORIFY SATAN THROUGH MY MUSIC? I SURE AS HELL DO! CONTEXT MAKES THE DIFFERENCE.

Intent is everything and I couldn't agree with his statements more myself.

Some thoughts as I reflect back on my research for this chapter echo the words of an internet writer I found named Johnny Marr:

> IN THE REALM OF CRACKPOT LITERATURE, FEW SUB-GENRES SURPASS ANTI-ROCK "N" ROLL LITERATURE IN SHEER QUALITY. LIKE THE FINEST FRINGE LITERATURE, THEY ARE SUFFUSED WITH PARANOIA, RABID PASSION AND A REFRESHINGLY ORIGINAL TAKE ON CONVENTIONAL LOGIC. THEIR PHILOSOPHY COMBINES THE BEST ELEMENTS OF FUNDAMENTALIST ZEALOTRY, COMMUNIST CONSPIRACY, AND BIZARRE PSEUDO SCIENCE... THE OPPOSITION TO ROCK "N" ROLL HAS A LONG HISTORY, PROBABLY STARTED WITH THE FIRST HIT. BOB (LARSON, EVANGELIST WRITER AND TALK SHOW HOST) POINTS STRAIGHT AT THE HORNED ONE, WRITING, "ROCK AND ROLL IS A PART OF THIS PLAN (SATAN'S) TO ACHIEVE A WORLD-WIDE MORAL DECAY." DRAWING ON NOEBEL, LARSON WARNS OF THE POWER OF THE BEAT. IT'S THE DEVIL'S BEAT, BORROWED FROM PRIMITIVE, HEATHEN RITUALS WHICH WHIPS DANCERS INTO A FRENZY. IT'S THE BEAT, THROBBING IN SYNC WITH THE BODY'S NATURAL RHYTHMS THAT HYPNOTIZES KIDS, TRIGGERS RIOTS, AND LEAVES THEM INCAPABLE OF MAKING SOUND MORAL DECISIONS AFTER THE DANCE. ACCORDING TO LARSON, "LYRICS OF TODAY'S ROCK SONGS ARE A LARGE PART OF THE TIDAL WAVE OF PROMISCUITY, ILLEGITIMATE BIRTHS, AND POLITICAL UPHEAVAL THAT HAVE SWEPT OUR COUNTRY."

Larson, the talk show host and author, gave warnings regarding youth centers, particularly in claims about Heavy Metal music and particularly the metal music of musician Ozzy Osbourne and of bands like Slayer, Black Sabbath, Judas Priest, Metallica, and Mega Death back in 1989. He has had the current High Priest of the Church of Satan on his show before to debate core issues and how they conflict with Christianity, and he warns "misguided" adolescents, when used excessively, under proper circumstances, the beat of rock is a force accommodating demonic possession and therefore is not worthy as a vehicle to communicate the gospel.

I find this heavily ironic, given my own position in Anton LaVey's Church. It was due to this fact that author Michelle Belanger requested my presence to join a discussion panel, for which I was asked to speak at a religious tolerance conference next to a pagan priestess and Father Bob Bailey of the Catholic

Dark Horizon Records catalog cover illustration by author.

Church. During this lengthy event we came to a mutual consensus that we all shared a far greater amount of common ground than anyone had previously believed. We talked and agreed on a surprising number of topics, and became pretty good friends who shared lunch and dinner before and after the lectures and classes at The Open House in Cleveland for House Khepereu in May of 2010. I explained Devil worship isn't Satanism at all and the convention attendees enjoyed my presentation for the next few hours and asked serious questions regarding religion and philosophy in context to today's issues.

However, not all people are as open minded on both sides of the fence as we were, if you look at people in our recent past. During this period of Rock and roll and the Devil, the Church of Satan, and heavy promiscuity examined by the media, religion in general, and the public masses, a new hysteria swept the land as the old fires long thought dead from the Great Inquisition grew once more. It was to rear its ugly head again in our time, known as SRA (Satanic Ritual Abuse) or the Satanic Panic era of the 1980s and 1990s.

Quintessentials. Courtesy Warlock Les Hernandez.

Quintessentials the Horror Never Ends Album. Courtesy Warlock
Les Hernandez

Quintessentials Pentagonal Revisionism. Courtesy Warlock Les Hernandez.

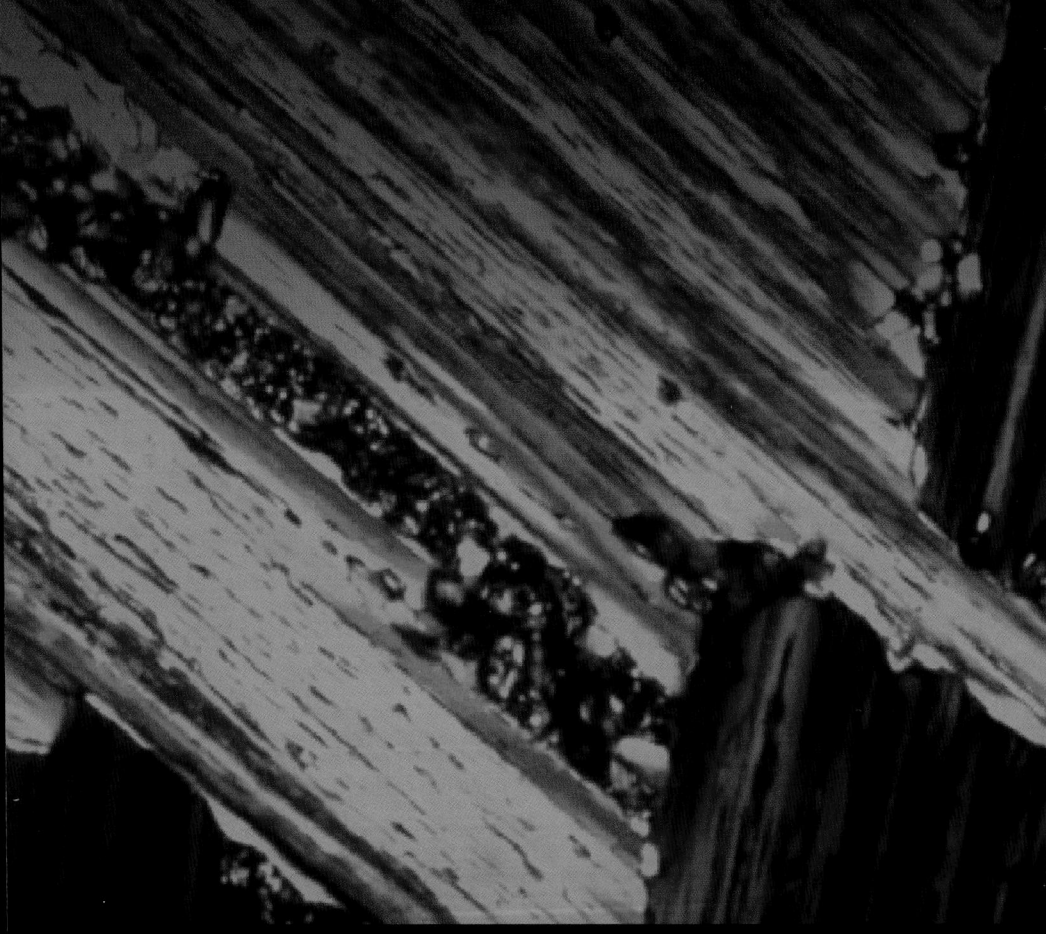

Chapter Six

Satanic Panic

The SRA panic, known as Satanic Ritual Abuse, ritualistic abuse, or organized sadistic ritual abuse, refers to a moral panic that originated in the United States in the 1980s. It repeated many of the features of historical moral panics and conspiracy theories such as the blood libel against Jews which date back to 30 A.D., the Knights' Templar of the Crusades, and the witch hunts of the sixteenth and seventeenth centuries writes Jeffery S. Victor in *Satanic Panic: The Creation of a Contemporary Legend.* Typically, wild and unfounded allegations of horrific acts by outsiders would include charges of cannibalism, child murder, torture, and incestuous orgies. This type of scapegoating continues to crop up every so many centuries. Torture and imprisonment were used by lynch mobs and judicial powers that be to coerce confessions from alleged criminals, which were later used to justify their execution.

Dark Candles. *Courtesy* The Ninth Gate Magazine *archives.*

As bewilderingly shocking as it is that such things happen still in our enlightened society, several things aided in creating this widespread epidemic. The establishment of Fundamentalist Christianity and political organization of the Moral Majority and the Anti-cult movement which spread notions on cults kidnapping our youth (especially infants), and misguided professionals who spoke out as authorities on repressed memory all added to the decade long hysteria.

The Modern Witch Hunt

In our modern age, Devil worship reached a fever pitch when hyped by media, especially when journalists such as Geraldo Rivera, who wrote the foreword to Jerry Johnston's sensational book, *The Edge of Evil: The Rise of Satanism in North America* added to the fire. Far worse yet was Rivera's own TV special *Devil Worship: Exploring Satan's Underground*, where he made unfounded claims about the supposed satanic threat in 1988. Later, the *Geraldo* and *The Oprah Winfrey Show* aired episodes involving followers of the Church of Satan who attempted to debunk it all as what it was – hysterical nonsense. Unlike many who followed his crusade, Mr. Rivera did publicly apologize for the mistakes and possible harm he caused innocent people by his accusations.

Many unjustly accused others of engaging in horrifying acts and satanic ritual abuse against children, aided in the witch-hunt by devoted therapists and pious police and prosecutor. At the same time, a group of "experts" on Satanism came forward, like evangelist and author Bob Larson and Michelle Smith who helped spread sensational stories of a worldwide organization of a satanic order bent on taking over the world. Christian groups, paranoid parents, and unethical professionals cashed in on the craze, making fortunes off books and tours, claiming the Devil was alive and well in every city in the United States. These unfounded satanic ritual abuses claims destroyed countless lives, as real charges of child abuse – one only need read *Paint it Black*, *Michelle Remembers* to see how crazy it all was. Dr. Lawrence Pazder, coauthor of *Michelle Remembers* recounted the supposed repressed memories of the author's wife, writing claims that Devil-worshippers have a conspiratorial network dedicated to ritual child sacrifice and world domination, to which the author adds his thoughts on drug cartels, and "kiddie porn." Via hypnotherapy (which he performed himself), the author dredges up the details of "Michelle's" experiences with a world-wide Satanic cult, and the author defines "ritualized abuse of children...repeated physical, emotional, mental, and spiritual assaults combined with a systematic use of symbols and secret ceremonies designed to turn a child against itself, family, society, and God."

Christian evangelists jumped on the bandwagon, and "therapists" began coincidentally "finding" similar tales buried in the subconscious with more and more patients, that is until Kenneth V. Lanning, Supervisor Special Agent Behavioral Science Unit National Center for the Analysis of Violent Crime, came forward and tore apart the façade endorsed by so many law enforcement lecturers. "The fact is that far more crime and child abuse has been committed by zealots in the name of God, Jesus, Mohammed, and other mainstream religion than has ever been committed in the name of Satan. Many people, including myself, don't like that statement, but the truth of it is undeniable," said Lanning, observing that murderers who attribute their crimes to commands from God far outnumber murderers who blame Satan, but no one has ever had reason to label their crimes Christian ritual sacrifices. Eventually, the whole "Satanic Panic" was debunked like any other urban legend, in part by Kenneth V. Lanning at the FBI.

I had the good fortune to interview Mr. Lanning, who is now retired, other than giving lectures on occasion, and he was a warm and cordial man who recalled that during his sixteen years investigating and researching the SRA that "… folklorists, historians, and secular educators have found that such occurrences are cyclical in nature." He explained that as he was approached by hundreds of prosecutors to explain his findings and "profile" a Satanist, he was more and more adamant in telling even local police who seized private alters and related belongings from a suspect's home when it was unrelated to the case being investigated. "You don't take a crucifix off a wall of a person you bring in," he told me he had yelled at the officer, "anymore than a bank robber is a criminal for being what his religion is, it doesn't make it a crime by that person's faith… It is ridiculous to profile people based on religion when it had nothing to do with the criminal act." He went on to tell me that far too often, people were judged based on what they were in that period, not what illegal activity they committed. Law enforcement reacted due to public fear and media hype, not based off of the law and the Constitution.

In still another venue, the book, *Selling Satan*, exposed the fraudulent claims of seminar leader Mike Warnke and Jeffery Victors *Satanic Panic*, but not before hundreds innocent individuals were nearly destroyed professionally. Law enforcement agencies, skeptical societies, and sociologists suddenly started to back pedal, as they examined this Christian-propaganda hoax and courts began to reverse decisions made against the accused.

Sean Sellers – Devil Child

On September 8, 1985, Sellers, when he was 16, shot and killed a convenience store clerk in Oklahoma City. According to the testimony of Sellers' best friend, Richard Howard, who was with him at the time of the murder, said that he killed Robert Bower because he "wanted to see what it feels like to kill somebody." Just a few days before, on March 5, 1986, Sellers shot and killed his mother, and stepfather, while they slept in their Oklahoma City home. Howard testified that just after the murders, Sellers had come to his house and told him that he had killed his parents. Howard, was initially charged with first degree murder also, but the state dismissed the charge and recommended that he be given a five-year suspended sentence in exchange for testimony against Sean. He and Howard were apparently attempting to rob the convenience store clerk, who had once refused to sell them beer, and the murders of his mother and stepfather occurred after they refused to let him date a girl he liked,

although at his trial, Sellers pleaded not guilty by reason of insanity and claimed he had no recollection of the murders, when later still he claimed his murders were motivated by satanic beliefs. At the trial, his defense argued Sellers was addicted to the game *Dungeons and Dragons* and had no control over his actions. Hardly a case of responsibility for the responsible by Church of Satan members – and it needs mention as to the difference as investigators found a copy of Anton LaVey's work in Sellers' room, claiming it was a motivating factor.

Sellers has achieved considerable fame as one of the nation's few juveniles sentenced to death, and his case is frequently cited by anti-Satanists as proof of their claims (see Bob Larson in the Bibliography). What is not taken into perspective is that Satanism and Devil worship are two entirely different ideologies as we learned in Chapter Three, The Devil's Champions. The 1989 book *Devil Child* provides a dramatic summary of the claims anti-Satanists make about satanic activity:

THOSE WHO CHOOSE TO BELIEVE THAT SATANIC PRACTITIONERS DO NOT INHABIT THEIR TOWN OR CITY, DO NOT SHOP IN THEIR GROCERY MARTS, DO NOT OCCUPY THE CAR IN THE PASSING LANE, MIGHT TAKE NOTE OF SOME FIGURES. IN 1976 THE NUMBER OF ACTIVE SATANISTS IN THE U.S. NUMBERED NEARLY HALF A MILLION. BY 1985 THAT FIGURE ALMOST TRIPLED. NO COMMUNITY IS UNTOUCHED. NO BOUNDARY IS UNCROSSED.

Sellers suffered from Multiple Personality Disorder or MPD (now known as Dissociative Identity Disorder) at the time of the murders; however, the Oklahoma Court of Criminal Appeals (OCCA) refused to consider the evidence. Clemency was denied on January 27 and the Oklahoma Pardon and Parole Board voted 5-0 to deny clemency to Sean Sellers. Dianna Craun, one of the jurors who sentenced Sellers to death, spoke on his behalf at the clemency hearing. She said that the jury was given two choices of sentencing: a life sentence (with the possibility of parole) or the death penalty. Dianna and the other jurors mistakenly thought that a life sentence would mean that Sean would serve seven to fifteen years in prison, and that this sentence was too lenient for the murders. She stated that the jurors did not honestly expect that Sean would ever be executed. "It is very obvious that he's found God, and God has changed his life," she told the parole board. "I was touched...and I truly don't want him executed."

During Sellers' incarceration, he warned people of the dangers of experimenting with the occult, in *An Open Letter to Satanists* where he says he was aware of Anton Lavey's ideology, stating,

> I was 15 years old when I became a Satanist. Today I'm 29. 15 was a lifetime ago. My concept of Satan and God back then was so different from what it is now. At 15 we really do think we know so much, but lock a man in a box for a few years alone, let him get to know himself, let him grow and look again at the world, and what he sees is a world very, very different from the one he perceived at 15. You know, I had *The Satanic Bible* practically memorized when I was 16. I'd read that book easily a hundred times. But I didn't understand why Anton LaVey wrote some of the things I had the good fortune to interview Mr. Lanning, who now retired other than giving lectures on occasion, and he was a warm and cordial man who recalled that during his 16 years investigating and researching the SRA that "...folklorists, historians, and secular educators have found that such occurrences are cyclical in nature." He explained that as he was approached by hundreds of prosecutors to explain his findings and 'profile' a Satanist, he was more and more adamant in telling even local police who seized private alters and related belongings from a suspect's home when it was unrelated to the case being investigated. "You don't take a crucifix off a wall of a person you bring in," he told me he had yelled at the officer, "anymore than a bank robber is a criminal for being what his religion is, it doesn't make it a crime by that persons faith...it is ridiculous to profile people based on religion when it had nothing to do with the criminal act." He went on to tell me that to far too often people were judged based on what they were in that period not what illegal activity they committed. Law enforcement reacted due to public fear and media hype, not based off of the law and the Constitution. he did. I didn't really comprehend Anton's ideology, his image of Satan or the Devil. That also took years.

It is clear, by his own admission, he comprehended little to do with the social contract most sane human beings exhibit, Satanist or otherwise. Unfortunately, many books, evangelists, and websites continue to hold Sellers up as a propaganda tool – an example of what a Satanist is, when in all reality, he was not even a self-described devil worshiper. He carried *The Satanic Bible* around at school to frighten people.

Further notation on Sellers, for anyone in the legal field, can be found on Westlaw or Findlaw databases (or a *Google* search of the case file): *Sean Richard Sellers vs. State of Oklahoma*, 809 P. 2d 676 (1991).

Some adolescents do develop eclectic behavior, like Sean Sellers, who murdered a convenience store clerk, his mother, and his stepfather — this does not prove the existence of a satanic coven, because Sellers developed his system of Devil worship on his own. The prevailing attitude and shoddy research of this movement is full of misleading statistics, rumor, and hack job sensationalism media claim "satanic/occult cult crimes thrives in America and this brand of public education is notorious for claiming satanic." Kenneth V. Lanning, reports in 1989 that, in various training materials and lectures, he has heard all of the following referred to as Satanism (pp. 63-64):

ASTROLOGY	THE NEW AGE MOVEMENT
BUDDHISM	ORDO TEMPLI ORIENTIS
CHANNELING	THE ORTHODOX CHURCH
THE CHURCH OF SATAN	PAGANISM, RAJNEESH
DEMONOLOGY,	ROCK MUSIC
FREEMASONRY	ROMAN CATHOLICISM
HARE KRISHNA,	ROSICRUCIANISM
HEAVY METAL MUSIC	SANTERIA, SCIENTOLOGY
HINDUISM	STONER GANGS
HOLISTIC MEDICINE	THE TEMPLE OF SET
ISLAM	TRANSCENDENTAL MEDITATION
THE KNIGHTS TEMPLAR	THE UNIFICATION CHURCH
THE KU KLUX KLAN	VOODOO
MORMONISM	THE WAY
NAZIS	WITCHCRAFT

If this catalog were to be taken literally, one would conclude that human culture has very little to offer that is *not* satanic. Specifically, Lanning wrote in 1992 the following:

IN 1983 AND 1984, WHEN I FIRST BEGAN TO HEAR STORIES OF WHAT SOUNDED LIKE SATANIC OR OCCULT ACTIVITY IN CONNECTION WITH ALLEGATIONS OF SEXUAL VICTIMIZATION OF CHILDREN (ALLEGATIONS THAT HAVE COME TO BE REFERRED TO MOST OFTEN AS "RITUAL" CHILD ABUSE,) I TENDED TO BELIEVE THEM. I HAD BEEN DEALING WITH BIZARRE, DEVIANT BEHAVIOR FOR MANY YEARS AND HAD LONG SINCE REALIZED THAT ALMOST ANYTHING IS POSSIBLE. JUST WHEN YOU THINK THAT YOU HAVE HEARD IT ALL, ALONG COMES ANOTHER STRANGE CASE. THE IDEA THAT THERE ARE A FEW CUNNING, SECRETIVE INDIVIDUALS IN POSITIONS OF POWER SOMEWHERE IN THIS COUNTRY REGULARLY KILLING A FEW PEOPLE AS PART OF SOME SATANIC RITUAL OR CEREMONY AND GETTING AWAY WITH IT IS CERTAINLY WITHIN THE REALM OF POSSIBILITY. BUT THE NUMBER OF ALLEGED CASES BEGAN TO GROW AND GROW. WE NOW HAVE HUNDREDS OF VICTIMS ALLEGING THAT THOUSANDS OF OFFENDERS ARE ABUSING AND EVEN MURDERING TENS OF THOUSANDS OF PEOPLE AS PART OF ORGANIZED SATANIC CULTS, AND THERE IS LITTLE OR NO CORROBORATIVE EVIDENCE. THE VERY REASON MANY "EXPERTS" CITE FOR BELIEVING THESE ALLEGATIONS (I.E., MANY VICTIMS, WHO NEVER MET EACH OTHER, REPORTING THE SAME EVENTS,) IS THE PRIMARY REASON I BEGAN TO QUESTION AT LEAST SOME ASPECTS OF THESE ALLEGATIONS.

Law Enforcement and Satanic Crime

Back in 1989, many police departments had specialized training, convincing the officers and investigators that various types of involvement in satanic belief relate to criminal behavior.

In the order of their criminality, these types are:

1) "Religious Satanists," members of organized churches including the Church of Satan, the Temple of Set, and the Church of Satanic Liberation, to whom little criminal activity has been linked;

2) "Experimentalists," youth who dabble in Satanism, heavy metal music, horror videos, fantasy role-playing games, and who have been tied to trespass, burglary, criminal damage, drug use, suicide, and homicide;

3) "Self-styled Satanists," sociopaths or psychopaths who justify criminal activity through a belief system centered in Satan;

4) "Satanic cults," groups of people, often with severe mental and behavioral problems, who are attracted to Satanism because it condones antisocial behavior;

5) "Orthodox satanic groups," intergenerational groups which pass their belief systems and coven structures to their children; criminal activities attributed to them include kidnapping, drug dealing, ritual child abuse, human sacrifice, and cannibalism.

There is no hard evidence to support the existence of any type of Satanist or their supposed criminal activities save for the fourth example and this is not "Satanism" but Devil Worship – two totally different schools of thought. Such criminal and antisocial behavior is contrary to the published philosophies of recognized satanic churches. Such bogus cult crime seminars did nothing more than fuel the new Inquisitions fires of fear while cashing in on lucrative speaking fees and notoriety in the growth industry the satanic lecture circuit became. FBI Agent Lanning added,

Some professionals, however, in their zeal to make American society more aware of this victimization, tend to exaggerate the problem. Presentations and literature with poorly documented or misleading claims about one in three children being sexually molested, the $5 billion child pornography industry, child slavery rings, and 50,000 stranger-abducted children are not uncommon. The problem is bad enough; it is not necessary to exaggerate it. Professionals should cite reputable and scientific studies and note the sources of information. If they do not, when the exaggerations and distortions are discovered, their credibility and the credibility of the issues are lost.

Role Playing Games and Satanic Panic

Several cases have been tried in the courts in which bereaved parents have claimed that their children's suicides were caused by heavy metal music, but a vast majority of them were pointing fingers at fantasy role-playing games like *Dungeons & Dragons* (*D&D*) and has also been accused of causing teenage suicides as well as a corrupting primer in occult and satanic practices, says Bob Larson in 1989. He describes such cases by a theory which he explains: "… beginning with heavy metal and *D&D*, these youths inevitably slide into satanic dabbling, with books like *The Satanic Bible* as their guides, and ultimately become criminals, even murderers." Of course, the case of *State of Louisiana vs. Bryan Wayne Widenhouse, 582 S. 2d 1274 (1991)* provides an example of the absurdness of the anti-role-player movement.

The following excerpt from Anson Shupe, entitled "Pitchmen of the Satan Scare," is from a professor in my hometown, published by the *Wall Street Journal* on Friday, March 9, 1990.

"ECONOMICS FUELS THE SPREAD OF THE FEAR OF SATANISM BEYOND THE POPULAR CULTURE OF ROCK MUSIC AND HORROR MOVIES TO PROFESSIONAL AUDIENCES. MANY MIDDLE-LEVEL EDUCATORS, HEALTH AND SOCIAL SERVICE WORKERS, AND LAW-ENFORCEMENT OFFICIALS ACROSS THE COUNTRY ARE REQUIRED TO ATTEND A NUMBER OF EDUCATIONAL WORKSHOPS EACH YEAR TO KEEP OR UPGRADE THEIR CERTIFICATIONS OR TO BE ELIGIBLE FOR RAISES AND PROMOTIONS," SAYS ANSON SHUPE, A PROFESSOR IN MY HOMETOWN IN AN ARTICLE PUBLISHED BY THE WALL STREET JOURNAL ON FRIDAY, MARCH 9, 1990. CALLED PITCHMEN OF THE SATAN SCARE, SHUPE GOES ON TO SAY THAT "JUST AS EX-SATANISTS HAVE SEEMINGLY COME OUT OF THE WOODWORK IN RECENT YEARS TO GIVE THEIR GRIPPING TESTIMONIES, SO ALSO THE ENTREPRENEURIAL EXPERTS OF SATANISM HAVE EMERGED. NOW THEY ARE OFFERING WORKSHOPS TO ENLIGHTEN SERVICE PROVIDERS. AS A RESULT, SATANISM HAS EMERGED AS ONE OF THE MOST POPULAR OFFERINGS IN SUCH CONTINUING EDUCATION. .."

Mr. Shupe is a professor of sociology at Indiana-Purdue University at Fort Wayne and is preparing a book on cult and Satanic phenomena in the U.S. Cook v. Cub Foods, Inc. 99 F. Supp. 2d 945 2000 UY.S. Dist. The plaintiff claimed *D&D* drawings on a bulletin board constituted attack on his religious beliefs. Court ruled that *D&D* was religiously neutral and found for the defendant.

It becomes apparent that a large number of offenders become Satanists after the fact in order to defend themselves at trial as Sellers did. "Stoners" or as Church of Satan hierarchy simply refer to them as "Psuedo Satanists" is a term which had been used in southern California since the early 1970s to describe a groups of youth who socialized together using drugs and alcohol, and listen to heavy metal music. In 1985, a few "Stoners" were tied to incidents of grave robbery, cemetery and church vandalism, as well as animal killings, usually cited as evidence of satanic crime.

The anti-Satanist ideology went so far as to say the lack of evidence was a conspiracy cover up, as Satanists have infiltrated police agencies and the government and added even more outrageous statements. The very lack of evidence has itself become the most powerful proof of their claims – no forensic evidence was found to support these claims.

The witch hunt around the period ended and police slowly backed off making those making loud claims seem foolish. Who would have thought that the fervor rampant in the Dark Ages would be given serious thought in huge scale in our day of rationalism and science, but it did. However, when speaking to the administrators, and consulting Satanic Panic, it certainly seems to be accepted that the 1992 FBI report found that hysterical claims of organized groups in the thousands of Satanists coordinating abuse and sacrifices were completely unfounded, and proved no member of The Church of Satan was involved in even the few cases that were true at the time or before. Sadly, most of the cases of troubled youths who happened to really get into trouble were in truth depriving the children of critical actions needed to deal with the problems that were real and needed to be dealt with.

LUCIFER

Chapter Seven

Sexuality and the Devil

Devil Come Courting, *Courtesy Warlock
Draconis, The Devil's Diary magazine archives*

To paraphrase writer Tony Crisp, our western culture has had a long history of struggle with its openness with sex, as bizarre as it may sound; at one time it was thought that to even dream of sex was a sign of the Devil's influence. In Freudian theory, each of us meets enormous resistances to meeting the very experiences or insights which would lead to healing. In this sense, the Devil or Satan embodies all our wants, needs, and desires that puritanical and uptight reactionists still claim we should all deny in ourselves.

Satan and Sex. Photo courtesy Old Nick Magazine.

Stanislav Grof (born July 1, 1931, in Prague, Czechoslovakia) is one of the founders of the field of transpersonal psychology and a pioneering researcher into the use of non-ordinary states of consciousness for purposes of analyzing, healing, and obtaining growth and insight into the human psyche. All the cultures in human history, except the Western industrial civilization, have held holotropic states of consciousness in great esteem. They induced them whenever they wanted to connect to their deities, other dimensions of reality, and with the forces of nature. They also used them for diagnosing and healing, cultivation of extrasensory perception, and artistic inspiration. They spent much time and energy to develop safe and effective ways of inducing them... The struggle with and fear of one's own natural drives – the resistances to accepting healthy changes – have a place in the archetype of the Devil or Satan. The Devil, as in the example in modern psychology, is usually connected with repressed natural drives, particularly sexual. The struggle with paternal authority or power within oneself is also often represented as the Devil. I agree with another observation of Crisp when he remarks, "If we change our code of conduct, we may meet the Devil because we release the previously unexplored aspect of ourselves." Of course, it only appears in the image of the Devil or Satan if we are frightened of this emerging aspect of ourselves, and/or come from a background whereby religious symbolism plays a crucial role.

Lucifer and Sexuality

As religions insist, "Free will is the traceable factor in the 'original sin.'" The original sin and sexuality has long been connected with the Devil, with the weakness of man succumbing to the power of feminine wiles in disobeying God by the eating of an apple, then both clothing themselves in shame. Among many deities, a serpent was worn, as they were emblems of healing power as well as death. Dragons and snakes were synonymous with both evil and the Devil, although in truth, the image of a snake biting its own tail was a mythological symbol of male and female, of dark and light, good and evil – a yin and yang long within pagan circles. The snake was carved in stone or drawn within the form of a crescent shape, tying the night with the moon, an attribute in the goddess Artemis, especially as she was a fertility goddess, the protector of wild beasts, and belonged to the night. Commonly, the snake was a phallic symbol, as were horns – another shape of the crescent moon, which is a fertility symbol.

One only needs to see old artwork of the Devil and draw the connection that the Devil has with sex, as he is often portrayed with an erect phallus, which in and of itself is a symbol of the power to create life. Both horns figuratively and the phallus directly are penetrating. Members of the court and the public spectators alike were voyeuristically eager to learn all the details of sexual relations between Devils and witches – and the tortured witches obliged them with the most intimate descriptions, such as claims that the Devil's penis was hard, made of a hard cold metal, like iron; his semen was ice-cold. Quoted a witch as saying that copulation was devoid of satisfaction and painful. In his Tableau, De Lancre gave some of the reasons:

MARIE DE MARIGRANE, A GIRL OF BIARRITZ AGED FIFTEEN YEARS, AFFIRMED THAT IT SEEMED THAT THE MEMBER OF THIS DEVIL FOR ITS FULL LENGTH WAS OF TWO PARTS, HALF OF IRON, HALF OF FLESH, AND SIMILARLY HIS TESTICLES; AND SHE TESTIFIED TO HAVE SEEN IT MANY TIMES AT THE SABBAT AS SHE DESCRIBED IT. FURTHERMORE, SHE HAD HEARD MANY WOMEN, WHO HAD SLEPT WITH THE DEVIL, SAY THAT HE MADE THEM CRY OUT LIKE WOMEN IN TRAVAIL WITH CHILD, AND THAT HE ALWAYS HELD HIS TOOL EXPOSED. PETRY DE LINARRE TESTIFIED THAT THE DEVIL HAD HIS INSTRUMENT MADE OUT OF HORN, OR AT LEAST IT LOOKED LIKE THAT, AND THAT IS WHY HE MADE THE WOMEN CRY OUT SO MUCH. ANOTHER WITNESSES ADDED FURTHER DETAILS OF THE DEVIL'S PENIS. THIS WAS GENERALLY SINUOUS, POINTED, AND SNAKE-LIKE, MADE SOMETIMES OF HALF-IRON AND HALF-FLESH, AT OTHER TIMES WHOLLY OF HORN, AND COMMONLY FORKED LIKE A SERPENT'S TONGUE; HE CUSTOMARILY PERFORMED BOTH COITUS AND PEDERASTY AT ONCE, WHILE SOMETIMES A THIRD PRONG REACHED TO HIS LOVER'S MOUTH.

Similar confessions from Lorraine were recorded by Remy in his Demonolatreiae:

> THE FEMALE WITCHES ALSO ALL MAINTAIN THAT WHEN THEY ARE LAID BY THEIR DEMONS, THEY CAN ADMIT, ONLY WITH THE GREATEST PAIN, WHAT ARE REPUTED THEIR TOOLS, BECAUSE THEY ARE SO HUGE AND RIGID. ALEXIA DRIGIE EXAMINED HER DEVIL'S PENIS WHEN IT WAS STICKING UP, AND SAID IT WAS ALWAYS AS LONG AS SOME KITCHEN UTENSILS WHICH THEN HAPPENED TO BE IN VIEW AND WHICH SHE POINTED OUT WITH HER FINGER; BUT THAT THERE WAS NOTHING WHERE THE TESTICLES SHOULD BE HANGING. CLAUDIA FELLET SAID SHE HERSELF HAD OFTEN EXPERIENCED SOMETHING FORCED INTO HER, SWOLLEN TO SUCH A SIZE, THAT NO MATTER HOW CAPACIOUS A VAGINA A WOMAN MIGHT HAVE, SHE WOULD NOT BE ABLE TO HOLD IT WITHOUT EXTREME PAIN. AND NEARLY ALL THE OTHER WITCHES COMPLAIN THEY ARE VERY UNWILLING TO BE EMBRACED BY THEIR DEMONS, BUT THAT IT IS USELESS TO STRUGGLE AGAINST THEM.

The relatively late dissertation of Johann Klein gave some of the most detailed accounts of the monstrous offspring of these unions. Satan's penis was bifurcate, that is to say, it was able to penetrate two orifices at once. Sometimes it was even trifurcate, able to penetrate mouth, anus, and vagina simultaneously. Marie de Marigrane, aged fifteen years, affirmed that she had often seen the Devil couple with a multitude of women, whom she knew by name claiming that it was the Devil's custom to have intercourse with the beautiful women from the front, and with the ugly from the rear. Another witness examined by De Lancre, seventeen-year-old Marguerite de Sare, testified that whether the Devil appeared as man or goat – he always had a member like a mule, having chosen to imitate that animal as being best endowed by nature; that it was as long and as thick as an arm... and that he always exposed his instrument, of such beautiful shape and measurements. The wishful basis of these descriptions would be obvious and even a bit silly if not for the fact that so many women (and even girls as young as eight to thirteen years) were put to death for supposedly having had intercourse with Devils. The minds of the Inquisitors were revealed, speculates Henry C. Lea, "The curiosity of the judges at witch trials... insatiable to learn all the possible details as to sexual intercourse, and their industry in pushing the examination was rewarded by an abundance of foul imaginations." Combined with the fact hysterical young women about to be burned produced most of the accounts, which theoretically could very well explain the erotic imaginations that projected whatever the torturers wished to hear.

Lust and the Watcher Angels

Theologians and demonologists were puzzled as to how demons, who were spirits, could have relations with humans; but nevertheless, it was a fact itself that was accepted, for it had the authority of the Bible and Church behind it. Augustine, in his De Civitate Dei, expounded Genesis declaring, "The sons of God came unto the daughters of men, they bare children to them." He was the first to consider fully "whether the angels, since they are spirits, are able bodily to have intercourse with women." Augustine inclined to the affirmative; although he denied that the angels of God so sinned. However, the famous book of Enoch referenced in the Bible was called The Three Books of Enoch, found in the Old Testament, The Grigori or Watcher Angels, as they are more known, were placed in charge of keeping an eye on mortals while assisting the Archangels building Eden. Watcher Angels descended to Earth and fell in love (or Lust) with the daughters of Adam and Eve. They bore children of them, half man, half angel, called the Nephilim, or giants. They were taught astrology and the production of war machines, as well as cosmetics. Perfume and makeup attributed to the beauty and lust of the descendants. A furious and vengeful God cursed the angels who he felt betrayed him, and transformed them into demons. Pope Benedict XIV, in De Servorum Dei Beatificatione, commented:

THIS PASSAGE HAS REFERENCE TO DEVILS KNOWN AS INCUBI AND SUCCUBI... FOR WHILE NEARLY ALL AUTHORITIES ADMIT COPULATION; SOME WRITERS DENY THAT THERE CAN BE OFFSPRING.... OTHERS, HOWEVER, ASSERTING THAT COITUS IS POSSIBLE, MAINTAIN THAT CHILDREN MAY RESULT, AND SAY THAT THIS HAD ACTUALLY OCCURRED, ALTHOUGH IN SOME NEW AND UNUSUAL WAY NOT ORDINARILY KNOWN TO MEN.

Satan's Sexual Minions

For most of the history of Christianity there are reports of Satan having sex with humans, while witches were thought by many to be the offspring who had inherited some of the Devil's powers. *Robbins' Encyclopedia of Witchcraft and Demonology* reads:

SUCCUBUS: A DEVIL IN FEMALE FORM, THE SUCCUBUS SPECIALIZES IN SEDUCING MEN. ALTHOUGH FEMININE IN MEANING, IN FORM THIS MEDIEVAL LATIN WORD SUCCUBUS, IS MASCULINE (BECAUSE DEMONS WERE SUPPOSEDLY SEXLESS); THE FEMININE FORM SUCCUBA [STRUMPET] IS OCCASIONALLY FOUND. SINCE WOMEN WERE ALLEGEDLY MORE LICENTIOUS THAN MEN, THE MALE INCUBI APPEAR MORE FREQUENTLY IN WORKS ON DEMONOLOGY; IT WAS SUPPOSED THAT INCUBI OUTNUMBERED SUCCUBI BY NINE TO ONE.

Another explanation of the succubus appeared in 1801, in *The Magus*, by author Francis Barrett, who felt a succubus was really a wood nymph, although he gravely agreed that Satan could himself appear as a young woman:

AND SEEING THE FAUNI AND NYMPHS OF THE WOODS WERE PREFERRED BEFORE OTHER [SPIRITS] IN BEAUTY, THEY AFTERWARDS GENERATED THEIR OFFSPRING AMONG THEMSELVES, AND AT LENGTH BEGAN WEDLOCKS WITH MEN, FEIGNING THAT, BY THESE COPULATIONS, THEY SHOULD OBTAIN AN IMMORTAL SOUL FOR THEM AND THEIR OFFSPRING; BUT THIS HAPPENED THROUGH THE PERSUASIONS AND DELUSIONS OF SATAN TO ADMIT THESE MONSTERS TO CARNAL COPULATION, WHICH THE IGNORANT WERE EASILY PERSUADED TO; AND THEREFORE THESE NYMPHS ARE CALLED SUCCUBI; ALTHOUGH SATAN AFTERWARDS COMMITTED WORSE, FREQUENTLY TRANSCHANGING HIMSELF, BUT ASSUMING THE PERSONS OF BOTH INCUBI AND SUCCUBI IN BOTH SEXES; FOR THEY CONCEIVED NOT A TRUE YOUNG BY THE MALES, EXCEPT THE NYMPHS ALONE.

The *Malleus Maleficarum* relates an incident that a man, in front of his wife and friends, was forced to have intercourse with a succubus. He kept at it three times; but when the succubus wanted to recommence, the man fell to the floor worn out. Even Holy men and women of the cloth struggled, and St. Victorinus, succumbed. St. Hippolyutus was once visited by a nude woman, but when he threw his bedding over her to conceal her nakedness, the woman became a corpse (which of course the Devil had animated to tempt him to sin).

Satan's Minions. Courtesy of Dark Moon Press. (Original painting *The Departure of the Witches*, 1878, by Luis Ricardo Falero.) *Courtesy Library of Congress.*

Myths and Animal Instincts

Authorities in the 1500s and 1600s stated that even when the Devil appeared as an animal or bird, especially serpent, goat, or raven, intercourse was possible. A certain Francoise Secretain admitted copulation with the Devil, sometimes as a black man, but also as a dog, cat, or fowl. Before they were burned, the Scottish witches at Borrowstones in 1679 testified to the commissioners how the Devil "would have carnal dealing with [them] in the shape of a deer, or in any other shape, now and then. Sometimes he would be like a stork, a bull, a deer, a roe, or a dog, and have dealing with [them]." One of these witches, Margaret Hamilton, was accused of having had "carnal copulation with the Devil in the likeness of a man, but he removed from [her] in the likeness of a black dog.

Another symbol of the Devil's sexual prowess and virility is the occasional presence of cloven hoofs or the hindquarters of a goat, as this animal was considered a symbol of sexuality. Ancient Egypt, at the temple in Mendes, the goat was viewed as the incarnation of the god of procreation. As a ritual of worship, the male priests would use female goats for sex, and the female priests would do likewise with male goats. During the Middle Ages, the goat was associated with the Devil as one of his preferred forms, often in connection with sexual deviance. Women under trial as witches were forced to confess that they had sexual contact with the Devil in the form of an animal, usually a goat.

The sexuality and physical power of a bull, stag and other horned creatures were traits of Pan and Dionysus also merged here, as did the debauchery of Greek orgies from both. There is a famous statue of the mythological satyr, Pan, using a goat for sex, which was found in Pompeii. In modern pornography, this theme carries over, most visible in the adult feature *Satyr* starring Jenna Jameson, which certainly shows that today's interest in myths, magic and sex has not waned. Indeed, the Devil makes an appearance in several adult movies, such as Michael Ninn's 2006 release called *Sacred Sin* filmed in rocker Eddie Van Halen's home, as well as an earlier work by the same director, *Forever Night*. A goat symbolizes uncivilized sexual impulses which we experience as evil because of their compulsive nature, and as author James Hillman writes about the Greek/Roman figure of mythology comes from our dark impulses – one of which "Pan is the goat-God and this configuration of animal-nature distinguishes nature by personifying it as something hairy, phallic, roaming and goatish," thus it is not that far of a stretch to see why early theologians adopted Pan's look into various aspects of the Devil being half man, half goat with a huge phallus. Pan has been subsumed into the image of the Devil, "complete with horns and leering grin." Very much as Levi the occultist wrote about Baphomet, he is the Great All begetter, where the energy of life itself arises (hence the erection of the half man along with female breasts.) Hillman recognizes that Christianity, in its obstinate denial of the gifts of both Pan and the Devil, leaves no other recourse for both archetypal figures other than to hide with psyche's shadow.

"Humans cast no shadow only at noon, only at the dazzle and zenith of his pride," he observes, "but noon is also Pan's hour, so that at our greatest height we are in danger of the greatest fall... Pan thus drives out civilized morality in rebellious panic, intoxication, and goatiness." In this way, Pan is very much alive, "but appears now as Lucifer's heir, from below and within, as the ambivalent 'prince of this world,'" bringing together the aspects of vitality and darkness, merging into the sinister and seductive archetype we imagine today.

Baphomet

Baphomet appears in many contemporary works of horror and fantasy fiction. H.R. Giger's bio-mechanical interpretations of Baphomet in his art in the mid 1970s as it appears in his first hardback book as well as the 2007 calendar depict a very accurate version, paying homage to Levi's illustration.

The most common and famous illustration was given to the world by the classical occultist, Eliphas Levi, and it first appeared in his work Rituel Et Dogme De La Haute Magie. Levi believed that Baphomet was symbolic of the Astral Light, which has roots in primordial matter. Levi was also insistent that there was a correlation between Baphomet and Pan. A recent film, *Pan's Labyrinth* depicts the best version on the silver screen I've ever had the pleasure to see, and certainly mixes aspects of

both together well. Some groups of Witches invoke this being during Sabbats to strengthen the link between themselves and the web of life. Baphomet is the All begetter and All devourer, merging man, animal and plant, and it is ever changing, ever growing and dying. It is mindless, only filled with a Dionysian will to grow, feed, mate, survive, and die, repeatedly. It is filled with the ecstatic joy of life and death, and exists inside every living being. The purpose for the invocations that the Witches and magicians do is to awaken this force and set it free.

Baphomet is usually depicted as a demon (per Levi's interpretation,) but often is depicted as a hermaphrodite. This Templar idol has been variously described as having a human skull for a head, as I found, having two faces, as a cat-like creature or alternately as a bearded head. The head worshipped by the Templars has been mentioned on a History Channel show, after the popularity of *The Da Vinci Code* craze hit. Sometimes it was thought to be a Goddess, although we may never know. In his book, *Supremely Abominable Crimes*, author Edman Burman presents the following information:

> A HEAD WITH ONE FACE OR TWO FACES, SOMETIMES BEARDED AND SOMETIMES NOT, MADE OF SILVER OR OF WOOD, A PICTURE OF A MAN OR OF A WOMAN, AN EMBALMED HEAD THAT GLOWED IN THE DARK OR A DEMON.

The idol was said to be the source of fertility and wealth. Baphomet makes a rare film appearance in the 1968 Hammer Horror film *The Devil Rides Out*. Baphomet is one of many demons popularly referenced in black metal music and related artwork, such as in the lyrics of the English band Venom and the American band Goatwhore.

We see many unique demons or monsters named Baphomet appear in computer and video games. *Doom II* and its sequel have at their final levels a creature alternately called Baphomet or the "Icon of Sin."

The plot of the video game Broken Sword is: The Shadow of the Templars involves a sect of Templars who worship Baphomet. He is a demonic patron in "In Nomine." Usually, this figure is described as a monstrous head, a demon in the form of a goat, a figure with the head of a goat and the body of a man, and was thought to symbolize the burden of matter from which arose the repentance for sin. The human hands formed a sign of esotericism to impress mystery upon the initiates and represented the sanctity of labor. Two lunar crescents, the upper being white and the lower black, represented good and evil, mercy and justice.

The lower part of the goat's body was veiled but expressed the mysteries; the universal generation is symbolized by the phallus. Being hermaphroditic, the female breasts were the symbols of maternity, toil, and of redemption.

Baphomet was affiliated with many great occultists and organizations over the centuries; The Knights' Templar, Levi, in works by Aleister Crowley, and Anton LaVey and his Church of Satan to name a few. Each person generally has his or her own personal opinion of what Baphomet represented. The Knights of the Templar looked upon the skull of Baphomet as being symbolic of personal wealth and fertility. Other than the goat's skull within the inverted pentagram, the other most common depiction of Baphomet is the illustration of the goat-headed man perching on a platform on tarot cards and a sundry of other illustrations.

The worship of Baphomet has survived since time immemorial, having been worshipped by the cult of Mendes in Egypt and the Bacchants of ancient Greece. The worship survived in some mystery cults during the Classic Period, and well into the Middle Ages. Some of the myths about Witches Sabbaths may well be distorted legends about the cult of Baphomet.

Today, magicians are actively interacting with Baphomet; and by invoking and worshipping Baphomet, they feel one may gain insight into the secrets of life, and feel its power. Baphomet is the sum of all life, and knows all its secrets and desires.

Levi called his image "the Baphomet of Mendes." He combined the images of the Tarot Devil card and the he-goat worshipped in the city of Mendes. It is unclear whether the Ancient Egyptian women had intercourse with the goat during religious rites for fertility, but the Catholic Church claimed this and it is possible that this is where the notion that the Devil had intercourse with witches came from. The goat or ram was used as the master of fertility and was celebrated as "copulator in Anep and inseminator in the district of Mendes," where women were blessed with children. During rituals, women danced naked before the image.

Levi's depiction, for all its fame, is not particularly authentic to the historical description from the Templar trials, although it is not unlike gargoyles found on several Templar and non Templar churches – or the vivid gargoyles added to Notre Dame de Paris about the same time as his illustration.

This "Sabbatic Goat" may have partially derived from the eighteenth to nineteenth century Spanish artist Francisco Goya, who painted a *Witch's Sabbath* in 1800 in which a group of seated women were offering their dead infant children to a seated goat.

Different theories exist as to the origin of the term, including from the Greek words "Baphe" and "Metis." The two words together would mean Baptism of Wisdom. A certain Dr. Hugh Schonfield, a scholar who worked on the Dead Sea Scrolls, believed that the word Baphomet was created with knowledge of the Atbash substitution cipher, which substitutes the first letter of the Hebrew alphabet for the last, the second for the second last, and so on. Baphomet rendered in Hebrew, after interpretation, becomes the Greek word Sophia, or wisdom.

Satanists from the Church of Satan use Baphomet as the name of their organization's sigil, a point-down pentagram enclosing a goat's head, surrounded by five Hebrew letters spelling out "Leviathan." The Hebrew letters at each of the points of the pentagram. starting from the lowest point. are to be read counterclockwise. Translated, this is Leviathan, a sea creature figuring in Judaic mythology. Leviathan is commonly associated with Satan, and the fourth book of *The Satanic Bible* is named the Book of Leviathan.

According to Magus Anton LaVey, Baphomet was one of the infernal names used as a key to call upon dark forces, saying that He delighted in committing blasphemy against the Golden Dawn Magicians "Satanifying" the angelic beings. He then divided *The Satanic Bible* into corresponding parts to the elements and crown princes of Hell as he felt appropriate. Baphomet was symbolic

of indulgence, a force, which can be summoned by mages, but it cannot be easily controlled. Although versions of the Sigil of Baphomet appear as early as the 1897 book *La Clef de la Magie Noire* by Stanislas de Guaita, the variant in common circulation today was designed for use by the Church of Satan, and is known as the Sigil of Baphomet. This variant is copyrighted by the Church of Satan and cannot legally be reproduced without permission. This could very well be basis for the Egyptian- Templar-Masonic and Crowley connection, which is my conclusion after researching the timeline of everything for this book.

Historically, Baphomet is thought to symbolize the burden of matter from which arose the repentance for sin. Of course, Crowleyites still maintain Baphomet is one of the names of their master, Edward Alexander "Aleister" Crowley, whose notorious character garnered him attention in the twentieth century. Crowley did sign many documents with this name, as well as other fanciful handles, such as "To Mega Therion," which is Greek for "The Great Beast." Crowley did not accept his contemporary, Eliphas Levi's, version of the evil-looking Baphomet as the object of the anti-Knights Templar accusations with Harpocrates, the Ram of Mendes. However, for the sixteenth major trump card of Crowley's Tarot deck, we find it depicts the Ram standing beneath a stylized phallus, as a friendly four-legged, multi-eyed animal-god, not a demonic half-human hermaphrodite.

A slanderous deformation of the Latinized "Mahomet," a Medieval Latin rendering of Muhammad, the name of the prophet of Islam is a possible explanation of the name of Baphomet being altered over time. During the era of the Crusades, European literature contained considerable misinformation and distortions against Islam and its prophet, such as the claim that Muslims worshipped a god called "Termagant." It is therefore possible that the name Baphomet represents one more such incident, and was coined by the enemies of Islam, and made deliberately to resemble "Mahomet" for propaganda purposes. (From *Promethean Flame*, by Corvis Nocturnum, Dark Moon Press.)

The Original Black Mass and Sexuality

During the Middle Ages and in the midst of the witch-hunt mania, witches were accused of participating in these ceremonies, largely from the writers of the manual on witch-hunting, the *Malleus Maleficarum*, describing the witch's Black Mass in detail, which is where we get the sacrifice of babies and the drinking of blood. It is generally believed today that the Black Mass and other such Devilish rituals never took place and the idea of them on such a large scale was merely an example of Church paranoia and propaganda. They especially have no place in today's world, as with modern Witchcraft, because most Neo-Pagan witches do not believe in the Devil.

Crowley's ritual for the O.T.O. (Ordo Templi Orientis) is a Thelemic Order that did a ritual known as the Gnostic Mass. It did have a vague resemblance to some elements of Black Mass, in particular a nude female serving as the ritual's altar and the sexual served as the template for modern day Wiccan branches – Gardenarian and Alexandrain witchcraft with their emphasis on unabashed human sexuality. In modern Satanism, it is an effort to pay homage to the creation of ideas, life, and the power of women – not at all a lecherous objectification. Despite all the history behind it, there is no set Black Mass ritual; rather the ceremony is a parody on the holy Catholic Mass. Supposedly, urine was at various times substituted for holy water, or wine. Black candles were used instead of white ones, while the priest would perform the Black Mass wearing black robes and make use of the symbol of a goat head (see Baphomet). Since Medieval times, the notion that a ritual or category of similar rituals that parody the traditional Christian Mass include common elements such as mocking the traditional mass by corrupting prayers or reciting them in reverse, while they would offer allegiance to the Devil defiling the cross and employing a nude female upon whom sex acts are often performed to serve as the ritual's altar, (see illustration in Chapter Four on the Church of Satan, photo courtesy of *Old Nick Magazine*.)

Parodies of the established Christian Mass are certainly nothing new and many of the original mockeries of the Mass penned in the Middle Ages were created for that reason only, simply as parodies. What is thought of

The Witches Sabbath by Luis Ricardo Falero.

as the first true Black Mass, in about 1500, the cathedral chapter of Cambrai held Black Masses in protest against their bishop. A priest in Orleans, Gentien le Clerc, was tried in 614-1615, confessed to performing the "Devil's mass" which was followed by drinking, and a wild sexual orgy. In 1647, the nuns of Louviers claimed that they had been bewitched and possessed, were engaged in Devil worship, and that they themselves had been possessed by demons and forced by chaplains to participate naked in satanic masses wherein the host was trampled underfoot and the cross defiled by bodily fluids or by insertion into the nuns' vaginas.

The peak for the Black Mass was reached in the seventeenth century during the reign of Louis XIV, who was accused of being lenient toward witches and sorcerers. There exists one notorious mass performed for the mistress of Louis XIV. Catherine Deshayes, known as La Voisin, a witch that read fortunes and sold love potions. She was able to acquire priests, probably also protesting the Church, to say these blasphemous masses, including the infamous Abbé Guiborg. The Marquise de Montespan who had sought the services of La Voisin to arrange the Black Mass because she thought the king was interested in another woman. While using Montespan as a naked alter, Satan and his demons of lust and deceit, Beelzebub, Asmodeus, and Astaroth, were invoked to grant Montespan whatever she desired. During the ceremony, a naked Marquise de Montespan served as

Goya's artwork, *The Witches Hour. Courtesy Library of Congress.*

Title illustration of *Praetorius' Blocksbergs Verrichtung* (w1668).
Courtesy Library of Congress.

Witches and Devil woodcut from the 1700s.
Courtesy Library of Congress.

Hexensabbat, chronicles of Johann Jakob Wick.

the altar for the perverted Mass while clutching two black candles, a detail which may have established the origin of this aspect in future Black Masses. Supposedly, while incense burned, the throats of children were cut, and their blood drained into chalices and mixed with flour to make the host, and the evil priest and the two women took part in an orgy. Afterward, the burned the corpses of the children were later burned in the furnace of La Voisin's home. When the scandal broke, they were brought to trial and confessions were gotten by means of torture. Total almost 246 people were arrested by order of the king. Among them were some of France's highest-ranking nobility. The thirty-six commoners were executed, including La Voisin who was burned alive in 1680 as a witch and Guiborg was imprisoned. Most of the nobility receive jail sentences, or exile to the countryside. Afterward, they burned the corpses of the children in the furnace of La Voisin's home.

During the nineteenth century, the Black Mass went into further decline. A London fraternal group call the Hellfire Club, was said to perform a Black Mass, but performed as a mocking and non-fatal ritual which served little more than an excuse for the hedonists to have their drunken sexual escapades.

Anton LaVey had once stated that "Black Mass is not used in the current day by Satanists, as Anton LaVey explained in an interview with Occult America, and talked about the original Black Mass in history as performances" (psychodramas at a time when people needed them). They had to express their opposition, their rebellion against an established church. Our rituals are suitably modified to express the needs of our particular era... (the) black mass is not the magical ceremony practiced by Satanists. The Satanist would only employ the use of a black mass as a form of psychodrama. Furthermore, a black mass does not necessarily imply that the performers of such are Satanists. "A Black Mass is essentially a parody of the religious service of the Roman Catholic Church, but can be loosely applied as a satire on any religion," and the High Priest went on to call it a redundancy, and it is "commonly misinterpreted that the Church of Satan has performed actual Black Masses, however using baby-fat candles and kissing the Devil's buttocks [Author's Note: both are common practices outlined in the chapter] would be both contradictory and hypocritical for a Satanist to do.

Satan, Sex and Film

The History of the Devil:
Clive Barker Style

In East Bay theatre company, played Ragged Wing's new staging of *The History of the Devil*. Clive Barker says his play is more than a courtroom drama, but also an investigation into humanity's inhumanity. "The Devil says, 'Listen, it's time for me to get my moment before the court again.' He's definitely appealing. Part of the interest is that the audience is essentially the jury. We get a bunch of arguments put before us, dramatized. Depending on your politics, you may find there are different choices made by different people."

Best known for his horror films like the *Hellraiser* series, bestselling novels, as well as dozens of films, novels, short stories, comics and published art collections, Barker's first artistic collaborations were in theatre. One of his earliest plays, *The History of the Devil* was staged in Liverpool, England, which was also Barker's birthplace. Written in the early 1980s and published in 1995 as part of a collection of plays called *Incarnations*, Barker wrote it for his own theatre, The Dog Company, with himself as director. "It really plays with a broad feel," Barker said. Theatre critic Clive Barnes called it "a cross between John Grisham and John Milton." With the alacrity of that early script, *The History of the Devil* ran for two years at the Edinburgh Festival, and toured Europe for over a year. The whole point about the play is, the Devil feels he has suffered enough and wants to go back to heaven to make his final bid for liberty. He requests to be tried on the understanding that if he is found guilty, he will return to hell. But the Devil argues that humanity is indeed culpable in many of his alleged crimes. If he can prove that, then he can go back to heaven... The play is then shown in seven parts, each a short flight through history, in which the Devil's identity changes radically," said Barker, "As long as we do bad things, we need someone to blame."

Pacts With The Devil, A Chronicle of Sex, Blasphemy & Liberation by S. Jason is well illustrated, and it is a good source of more information, as is *Satanic Sexualis, an Encyclopedia of Sex and the Devil*, by Candice Black.

Angel Heart

In this film, Robert De Niro plays Lucifer – in this case specifically, Luis Cyper, with a masterful performance who leads Harry Angel (Mickey Rourke) to his own horrible discoveries about his past, his relationship with the Devil, and the deal he made in the name of greed, vanity, and power.

This film is noteworthy outside of the script itself as Lisa Bonet was kicked off *The Cosby Show* because of her part for her intense sexual scene.

The Devil Inside Her

This film is set in England, 1826, full of sex and satanic terror, takes a look at social class, the subjective nature of good and evil, and a poke at both politicians and religious authorities. Faith, an innocent, loves Joseph the gardener, but her domineering father forbids them to be together. Hope, Faith's sister, lusts after the same man, selling her soul to the Devil. The ritual and following ritualistic are cinematically inspiring.

The Devil in Miss Jones

In 1973, Gerard Damiano's *The Devil in Miss Jones* – Damiano working under the pseudonym Jerry Gerard – the director of *Deep Throat*, depicts a lonely thirtyish woman, Justine Jones, (acted by Georgina Spelvin) who kills herself. She finds herself in limbo, awaiting hell and she meets the Devil and is faced with an eternity in Hell. She imposes the hypothetical premise "If I had my life to live over, I would live a life consumed, engulfed, impassioned by lust!" Soon in the days that carnal pleasure commence, with Miss Jones seeking every imaginable form of pleasure back on earth, she takes on all comers. She finally finds herself transported to a cubicle of hell with an impotent man (Gerard Damiano, under the name of Albert Gork) who has no interest in sex at all.

Justine Jones, in part two filmed in 1982, is frustrated in hell. She makes a sexual deal with the Devil himself to earn a return to earth as an immortal human. However, in earning her escape, Lucifer falls in love with her, and he tries to place her soul in bodies on earth that are increasingly removed from opportunities for sex, in order to jealously deny her the one thing she craves. *The New Devil in Miss Jones* made the Best 2005 Porn Movies list due in part to infamous porn actress, Jenna Jameson. Jenna took matters into her own hands by putting her spin on this remake.

The Devil Inside Her, 1977, and the famous John Holmes last film was one of the most prolific male porn stars of all time. Old Nick takes the lead in *The Devil In Mr. Holmes* in 1974 with the famous John Holmes, one of the most prolific male porn stars of all time. His last film, which was *The Devil Inside Her, 1977*, features *Holmes as well*.

Other pornographic films such as *Cult of Sadists, Rites of Uranus, Lucifer's Lust*, and scores of others can be found if one searches for them.

Nude for Satan

Nude for Satan has to be one of the poorest quality B movies films I've ever endured. The story has a couple involved in a car accident. The doctor leaves the girl at the accident scene, leaves to go to a spooky castle for help. Later, the young lady goes looking for the doctor, and eventually finds her way to the same castle. Poor special effects, bad make-up, quite a few nude actresses litter the screen. Other lower grade pornographic films such as *Cult of Sadists, Rites of Uranus, Lucifer's Lust,* and scores of others can be found.

Club Satan: The Witches' Sabbath

Back when I published *The Ninth Gate Magazine*, I interviewed Shane Bugbee, a former priest in the Church of Satan who wrote and directed *Club Satan: The Witches' Sabbath*, a film featuring an actual Satanic black mass and starring black metal legends DARK FUNERAL, as the Devil's Disciple. Shane, the last ordained reverend by Anton LaVey in 1996, says "I was the last one ordained by LaVey before he died… When that happened, I was really honored, but I didn't give a shit. I don't care. I don't want to put a label on me at all. The Church of Satan really is for people that are non-joiners. They don't want labels. We are individuals." Shane began working with his old friend musician/pornographer, Matt Zane, of the band Society 1 and the adult production company Extreme Associates. Their first major event together was "666 Eve" – an orgy of metal music mixed with bloodletting and pornography, held in Los Angeles to celebrate the infernal holiday of June 6, 2006. The festivities included appearances from Extreme Associates starlet Lizzy Borden, Society 1, Headsick Pinups and everything imaginable – the DVD filmed at the event was dubbed "too hardcore" for many film critics to review. The second project Shane had in mind was an adult film. Not just any old sex fest, Shane was determined to make the most truly satanic one ever imaginable.

"I was just talking with Matt and I said, 'Man I've always wanted to do this porno,'" Shane said. "He's like, 'Oh, they'll never do that in porn.'" Despite the doubts, Matt's cousin Rob Black, agreed to work with Reverend Bugbee, owner of Extreme Associates. Together, they combined forces to create the publication Extreme Times and the adult video *Club Satan: The Witches Sabbath*. *Extreme Times*, edited and designed by Shane, made its debut at the expo. "Stand up for what you believe in," a free publication, covers the adult industry, extreme art, music and entertainment. The first issue featured a pinup of Lizzy Borden, announcements of upcoming Extreme Associates projects, and a Cooking with Porn Stars. This was Shane's directorial debut as a director of porn, written by him and his wife. This feature also is the debut of actors Paris and Zane together, with guest appearance of black metal band Dark Funeral.

When Shane discovered a long list of obscenity charges that had been thrown at Extreme Associates, he knew the black mass erotic masterpiece he had always envisioned wouldn't be censored by them. Rob Black has been fighting ten counts of obscenity since 2003. Years in court and spending untold thousands of dollars, Black continues to engages the case in court. In the face of charges pending, Extreme Associates presses ever onward, undaunted. As one can see in his promotional poster for *Club Satan*, it certainly looks as though it lives up to the boast of "carnality that most men refuse to believe even exists… This film is not for the weak; it should be viewed only by the virile and strong… This is the last taboo in porno," Shane said. "As 70ish, fun and horrific as it looks, this is one of the last taboos. They don't mix Satanism and porno. They say this is what the right wingers will go after. This is what they will persecute." Adding that the film is essentially horror porn and it's more of a sarcastic statement than an expression of true Satanism. "It's got a lot of blasphemy," Shane said. "The black mass in the Church of Satan is about exorcising demons. I had never done a mass before at all. I'm a Church of Satan priest that doesn't really believe in that. But I do have a strong disdain for organized religion of any kind, so it was nice to do the black mass. Stuff like smashing a cross, desecrating and doing blasphemous things kind of gets that stuff out of your system. And it did. It was fun to do as a filmmaker, but it was also fun in general. When I left I felt a lot better."

Old Nick Magazine

I was asked to partake in an interview for the October 2009 *Penthouse* as a member of the Church of Satan, and yet, the occasional men's magazine interview with sex and Satan is not so rare as one might think. I located the publisher of *Old Nick Magazine*, who jokingly refers to himself as Playboy with horns, and the mysterious gentleman was obliging enough to answer some questions for me.

What inspired *Old Nick Magazine*, I had asked. The publisher replied, "It became apparent to me that there was a void in men's Satanic entertainment. There are many fine publications, like yours, however, there lacked a sophisticated and titillating '*Playboy*-Esque' type magazine that celebrated the pure art of fine gentlemanly indulgences, lovely pulchritude and of course of all with a dark bent!"

Old Nick Magazine. Courtesy of Old Nick Magazine (2009).

Sexuality is an integral part of our carnal nature. Do you think it is as big a taboo now, with the changes in society – the fact America is slowly becoming more European, in being less shocked at nudity, sex? I asked. The suave and witty reply from my favorite magazine publisher was, "Sex will always carry with it some sense of taboo in our Judeo-Christian dominated society. I say let's embrace that – it's what makes the lust, the chase and the bedding of one's object so deliciously exciting! This is what Old Nick embraces – the tension of the tease and the ultimate release. The French call orgasm, Le Petite Morte – the little death, the ultimate release from wonderful sexual tension. Without taboo, there would be no tension. That's very satanic. We've received tremendous response from the Satanic community as well as from the fringe who embrace the dark aesthetic. Comments say that this is the type of men's magazine long overdue and it hits the mark for the alien elite. Men want to return to the times of the polished gentlemen who love wine, women, and song. I can only see our readership growing by leaps and bounds!"

High Priest Peter Gilmore agrees in his matter-of-fact thoughts. He is clear and direct to the skeptic stating, "Satanism is based on human nature, affirming the inborn character of the carnal types of humans... Prior to the founding of the Church of Satan, there was no form of religion that addressed this portion of our species. Carnal people have no need to seek acceptance from some higher power, whether it be a deity or a dictator. We aren't spiritual at all, and see all mysticism as childish superstition. We who embrace our fleshly nature revel in the joys of the body and the mind. Fine food, exemplary sex, excellent literature, exciting music—we are gourmets in the buffet that is life. We don't deny ourselves pleasures, but we also don't overdo them. The primary point is to indulge in what pleases us, but not to allow such pursuits to become compulsions that control us. Satanists are not addicts, are not sex maniacs, are not gluttons—we find balance in healthful pursuit of all that we enjoy. It is all about getting the most out of our lives. Carnal people don't just pursue happiness—they have it."

South Park

South Park creators Trey Parker and Matt Stone came up with the idea of Satan and Saddam Hussein being lovers on the set of BASEketball, where they would attempt to impress girls by improvising scenes between the two characters, one assuming the role of Satan and one of Saddam. This cartoon takes great delight in poking fun of the decaying values American. Satan is often portrayed in other media; he is depicted in the film *South Park: Bigger, Longer & Uncut*, where he is soft hearted and homosexually romantic with Saddam Hussein. Shocking? Yes. But hardly the vile destroyer of all mankind.

Satan, by Jean Jacques Feuchere (ca 1836). *Courtesy Library of Congress.*

political force in western culture, so too did the power of Satan. Near the end of *The History of the Devil* and the idea of Evil, Paul Carus asks of his reader, "Is not evil the product of mere illusion? Is it not a relative term which ought to be dropped as a one-sided conception of things?"

Of all the iconic images I have written about, I enjoyed exploring the Lucifer most of all. Of all possible figures to have layers of meaning behind, he is perhaps the most complex and powerful, yet the most human of them all. The evils bestowed on this enigmatic trickster from so many religions – from ancient myths and to cultures and legends – he continues through the ages to evolve in both appearance and even slightly in nature. The Devil is a necessary rebel, an adversary that people need as the ultimate villain, giving us a symbol. From Milton's pen and others like him, our sympathy to his martyrdom became realized, and loathing mixed to form a more complex character for art and literary works yet to come.

viable opponent to their beliefs, and despite my own personal thoughts on the matter, it all comes down ultimately to one's own world view. On one hand, he exists in the mind of the beholder, in another, not at all save the power we as a collective whole give to him. Educated people from either side of the fence will argue reality with no tangible empirical evidence and thus his existence or lack thereof is simply a philosophical-religious one, not a direct threat of our daily existence like that of nature's natural catastrophes or mankind's own horrors perpetrated on one another. Our own individuals experience with "evil," whether real or imagined, applies to us by way of life's conditions. It is socially destructive to give "the Devil" too much blame as that would take away the culpability of us – the human race – for our decisions. Believers as a whole may then forget that if an all powerful "good" exists with all control, then responsibility of the cause is also in its hands. Religion must face this

Afterword

dilemma or lose followers due to lack of comfort on blind faith, as a "good" cannot be reconciled with horrors allowed to continue from of war and genocide killings. If a being such as the traditional Satan did indeed exist, willfully causing harm to all mankind in retribution for whatever imagined wrong, is it not hypothetical to speculate such two powerful cosmic forces could not have reached a solution eons ago, one might imagine.

As with civilization and the mores and morals we exist by, the figure of Lucifer will always be reshaped as the embodiment of both evil and satire alike as he was during the Romantic period, as cynical free thinkers added aspects upon this symbolic character. Secular Humanists further drew the Devil with scientific skepticism and materialism where he exists solely as a symbol and less and less a real threat to anyone other than fundamentalists. A sardonic and quintessential gentleman, he will continue to remind us as Al Pacino said it best in *The Devil's Advocate*, "I don't make people do anything, it's all free will." We as fallible human beings will always require concepts, symbols, and rituals to get deeper in touch with our own existence and our place in the universe, and Old Nick certainly fills many needed gaps. If Lucifer did not exist, we surely would have created him regardless, for only he could force us to squarely face the opposition of stagnation and the preconceived ideals of right and wrong, oppression and total freedom.

Personally, I enjoy this archetype as the Romantic embodiment of a noble anti-hero, who pushes us towards new heights in rebellious yet creative ways, and sensual enjoyment of life's experiences. As an artist and writer, I have a special place for such an inspiring symbol to draw upon as I continue to evolve. I quote Arron Ross from "The Devil and the Pathology of History" where he says, "For one to obtain real freedom, society must finally come to grips with its own problems, our very human impulses once embodied in the Devil." Only by realizing that evil comes from within people and not any outside influence, can the scapegoat truly be hurled over the cliffs to its final death. The slowness of this process makes it nearly impossible to verify, but I believe that the human race is indeed engaged in it. However limited in the grand scale of things, when one looks at the human race as a whole, it is ultimately up to us as individuals to decide what direction our lives go in and follow through with passion, effort, and everything we have within us to shape it, and not place blame nor success on anyone or anything other than on ourselves, even the Devil.

Perhaps, even especially the Devil.

Bibliography

Abyeta, Suzanne and Forest, James (1991, December). *Relationship of role-playing games to self-reported criminal behaviour. Psychological Reports*, 69, 1187-1192.

Barton, Blanche *The Secret Life of a Satanist: The Authorized Biography of Anton LaVey.* Feral House publishing (1992).

Best, Joel. 1991. *Endangered Children in Antisatanist Rhetoric.* Pp. 95-106 in *The Satanism Scare.* Edited by James T. Richardson, Joel Best, and David G. Bromley. New York: Aldine de Gruyter.

Black, Candice. *Satanica Sexualis: An Encyclopedia of Sex And the Devil.* Wet Angel Books, (2007).

Bromley, David G. 1991. *Satanism: The New Cult Scare.* Pp. 49-72 in *The Satanism Scare.* Edited by James T. Richardson, Joel Best, and David G. Bromley. New York: Aldine de Gruyter.

Bromley, David G. (1991, May-June). *Satanic cult scare. Culture and Society*, 55-66. Alta Miri Press.

Carus, Paul. *The History of the Devil and the Idea of Evil From the Earliest Times to the Present Day.*

Cardwell, Paul, Jr. (1999). Comment on Leeds (1995). *Cultic Studies Journal*, 16:2, 197-203.

Curran, Hugh. 1992a. *Comment Gets Ornament Out of Wendy's: Someone Thought It Might be Satanic. Anchorage Daily News.* December 23.

————. 1992b. *Wandering Star Finds Safe Home: Eagle River Church Rescues Satanic Holiday Ornament. Anchorage Daily News.* December 24.

Daniels, S. 1989. *Satanic Beliefs, Criminal Actions.* Arlington, VA: International Association of Chiefs of Police. Unpublished.

Dawkins, Vicky L. and Nina Downey Higgins. 1989. *Devil Child.* New York: St. Martin's Press.

Doto, Pamela. 1991a. "Witches at the Mall: High Priestesses Hand Out Answers and Baked Goods." *Anchorage Daily News.* April 26.

Enge, Marilee. 1990. "Satanism Course Loses Endorsement." *Anchorage Daily News.* September 7.

Ewing, Charles Patrick. 1990. *When Children Kill: The Dynamics of Juvenile Homicide.* Lexington, MA: Lexington Books.

Finkelhor, David, Gerald Hotaling, and Andrea Sedlak. 1990. *Missing, Abducted, Runaway, and Thrownaway Children in America.* Washington, DC: Office of Juvenile Justice and Delinquency Prevention.

Hicks, Robert D. 1990. *In Pursuit of Satan: The Police and the Occult.* Buffalo, NY: Prometheus Books.

Hicks, Robert (1989). *Satanic cults: a skeptical view of the law enforcement approach.* Richmond, VA: Department of Criminal Justice Services. A criminologist looks at police handling of satanic panic and effect.

Gilmore, Peter H. 2008. *The Satanic Scriptures.* Scapegoat Publishing.

Jamra, Robert J. *The Church of Satan.* Los Angeles: Church of Satan, n.d. Photocopied.

Jenkins, Phillip. 1992. *Investigating Occult and Ritual Crime: A Case for Caution.* Police Forum (Academy of Criminal Justice Sciences Police Section). January.

Johnston, Jerry. 1989. *The Edge of Evil: The Rise of Satanism in North America.* Dallas: Word Publishing.

Lyons, Authur *Satan Wants You: The Cult of Devil Worship in America,* Mysterious Press, June 1, 1988.

Lanning, Kenneth V. "Investigator's Guide to Allegations of 'Ritual' Child Abuse," Behavioral Science Unit, National Center for the Analysis of Violent Crime, Federal Bureau of Investigation, FBI Academy, Quantico, Virginia 22135, 1992.

Lanning, Kenneth V. 1989. *Satanic, Occult, Ritualistic Crime: A Law Enforcement Perspective.* Police Chief 56(10): 62-84.

Lanning, Kenneth V. (1989, October). *Satanic, occult, ritualistic crime: a law enforcement perspective.* Quantico, VA: National Center for the Analysis of Violent Crime. Satanic panic viewed by an FBI Supervisory Special Agent and Academy instructor.

Larson, Bob. 1989. *Satanism: The Seduction of America's Youth.* Nashville: Thomas Nelson.

LaVey, Anton S. 1969. *The Satanic Bible.* New York: Avon Books.

LaVey, Anton S. *The Satanic Rituals: Companion to The Satanic Bible*. New York: Avon Books. 1976.

LaVey, Anton S. *The Satanic Witch*. Avon Press, 1976.

LaVey, Anton S. *The Devils Notebook*. Fereal House, 2000.

Nathan, Debbie *Satan's Silence : Ritual Abuse and the Making of a Modern American Witch Hunt*. Basic Books, October 3, 1996.

Nocturnum, Corvis. 2005. *Embracing the Darkness*; *Understanding Dark Subcultures*. Dark Moon Press.

Nocturnum, Corvis. 2007. *Promethean Flame*. Dark Moon Press.

Masello, Robert *Fallen Angels...and Spirits of the Dark*, Perigee Trade; 1 edition, October 1, 1994.

Masello, *Robert Raising Hell: A Concise History of the Black Arts* – and *Those Who Dared to Practice Them*. Perigee Trade; 1st edition. October 1, 1996.

Messadie, Gerald, *A History of the Devil*. Kodansha USA, November 17, 1997

Moynihan, Michael (and) Soderlind, Didrik. *Lords of Chaos: The Bloody Rise of the Satanic Metal Underground* New Edition. Feral House, 1st edition, April 1998.

Paradise, Matt G. *Bearing The Devil's Mark*. Purging Talon Publishing, 2008.

Passatino, Gretchen, Bob Passatino, and Jon Trott. 1989. *Satan's Sideshow*. Cornerstone 18(90): 23-28.

Raschke, Carl A. 1990. *Painted Black: From Drug Killings to Heavy Metal : The Alarming True Story of How Satanism Is Terrorizing Our Communities*. San Francisco: Harper & Row.

Rahn, Otto *Lucifer's Court: A Heretic's Journey in Search of the Light Bringers*. Inter Traditions, 2008.

Richardson, James T. *Satanism in the Courts: From Murder to Heavy Metal*. New York: Aldine de Gruyter. 1991.

Richardson, James T., Joel Best, and David Bromley. 1991. *Satanism as a Social Problem*. Pp. 3-17 in *The Satanism Scare*. Edited by James T. Richardson, Joel Best, and David G. Bromley. New York: Aldine de Gruyter.

Rivera, Geraldo. 1988. *Devil Worship: Exposing Satan's Underground*. NBC television documentary. October 25.

Pagels, Elaine (1995). *The Origin of Satan*. Vintage; Reprint edition.

Rebhorn Wayne A. *The Humanist Tradition and Milton's Satan: The Conservative as Revolutionary, Studies in English Literature, 1500-1900*, Vol. 13, No. 1, The English Renaissance, 1973.

Rudwin, Maximilian. 1970. *The Devil in Legend and Literature*. Open Court.

Russell, Jeffrey Burton. *Lucifer: The Devil in the Middle Ages*. Cornell Paperbacks, 1986.

Russell, Jeffrey Burton. *The Devil: Perceptions of Evil from Antiquity to Primitive Christianity*. Cornell Paperbacks, 1987.

Russell, Jeffrey Burton. *Satan: The Early Christian Tradition*. Cornell Paperbacks, 1987.

Russell, Jeffrey Burton. *Mephistopheles: The Devil in the Modern World*. Cornell Paperbacks, 1990.

Russell, Jeffrey Burton. *The Prince of Darkness: Radical Evil and the Power of Good in History*. Cornell Paperbacks, 1992.

Russell, Jeffery Burton *The Devil: Perceptions of Evil from Antiquity to Primitive Christianity*. Cornell Paperbacks, 1987.

Sass, James D. 2008. *Essays In Satanism*. LuLu Publishing.

Sass, James D. 2008. *The Anti-Christ: Curse Upon Christianity*. LuLu Publishing.

Sills, Donald N. 1990. "BeDeviling Questions About Workshops." *Law Enforcement News*. December 15.

Smith, Michelle and Lawrence Pazder. 1980. *Michelle Remembers*. New York: Congdon and Lattes.

Spencer, Judith. 1989. *Suffer the Child*. New York: Pocket Books.

Stratford, Lauren. 1988. *Satan's Underground: The Extraordinary Story of One Woman's Escape*. Eugene, OR: Harvest House.

Steffon, Father Jeffrey *Satanism: Is it Real?* Servant Publishing, 1992.

Trostle, Lawrence C. 1992. *The Stoners: Drugs, Demons, and Delinquency*. New York: Garland Publishing.

Truzzi, Marcello. 1974a. *Definition and Dimensions of the Occult: Towards a Sociological Perspective*. Pp. 243-256 in On the Margin of the Visible. Edited by Edward A. Tiryakian. New York: John Wiley & Son.

————. 1974b. *Witchcraft and Satanism*. Edited by Edward A. Tiryakian. New York: John Wiley & Son.

Victor, Jeffrey S. 1993. *Satanic Panic*. Open Court.

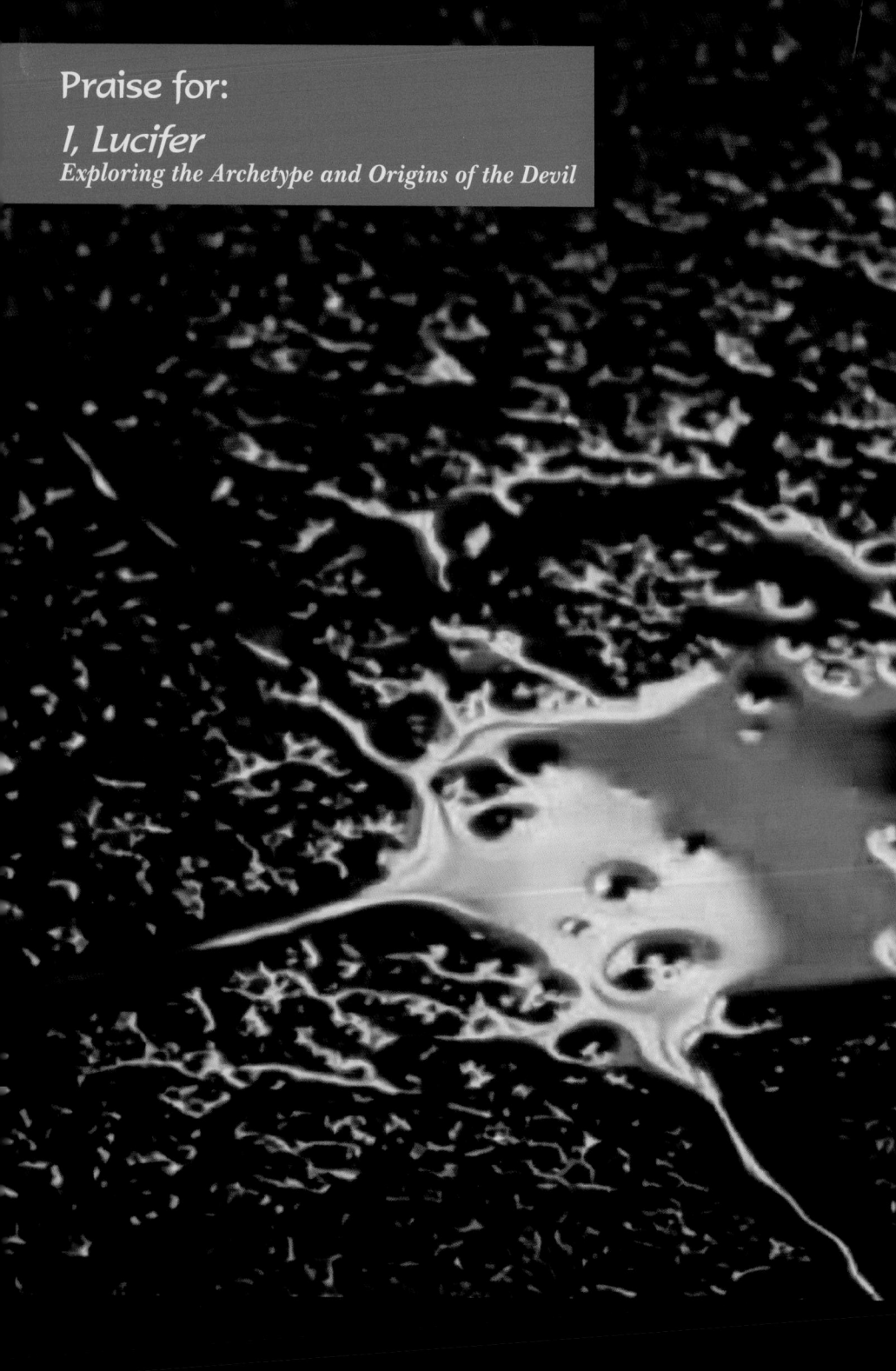

Praise for:

I, Lucifer
Exploring the Archetype and Origins of the Devil

CORVIS NOCTURNEM HAS DONE AN
ADMIRABLE JOB TRACING THE GENEALOGY OF
THE DEVIL FROM PRE-CHRISTIAN MYTHOLOGIES,
THROUGH THE WITCH-HUNTS OF EARLY MODERN
EUROPE, AND INTO THE SATANIC PANIC OF THE
MODERN ERA. I, LUCIFER IS A TRULY AMBITIOUS
PROJECT."

~ Jospeh Laycock, PhD
Boston University, 2011 Religion
and Society
Author of *Vampires Today: The Truth
about Modern Vampirism*

CORVIS NOCTURNUM HAS, WITH THIS BOOK, GIVEN THE READER A
WHOLE NEW WAY OF LOOKING AT THE DEVIL. I. LUCIFER: EXPLORING
THE ARCHETYPE AND ORIGINS OF THE DEVIL, IS IN MY OPINION THE
MOST COMPREHENSIVE LOOK AT THE CREATION AND EVOLUTION OF THIS
KEY DEMONIC FIGURE, WHO HAS FOR SO MANY GENERATIONS FRIGHTENED
AND CAPTIVATED MANKIND'S IMAGINATION, TO DATE. THIS IS NO SMALL
STATEMENT ON MY PART. I TOO AM ONE WHO HAS, WITH MY OWN WRITINGS,
SPENT MUCH TIME VISITING WITH AND STUDYING THIS CHARACTER OR
CHARACTERS THAT IS SATAN, BELIAL, LUCIFER, ETC. HOWEVER, THIS BOOK
TAUGHT EVEN ME A THING OR TWO NEW ABOUT THE DEVIL.

~Hydra M. Star, fiction writer and columnist
Belialian Woman for *Horrotica Magazine*

Cemetery Gates:
Death and Mourning through the Ages:

DYING IS NO LONGER A PART OF OUR POLITICALLY AND SOCIALLY CORRECT SOCIETY. THE RITES OF DEATH, ONCE KNOWN BY THE ENTIRE TRIBE HAVE BECOME HIDDEN SECRETS THAT TODAY FILL THE HEARTS OF MAN WITH DREAD.

AS WITH HIS PREVIOUS WORKS, CORVIS NOCTURNUM NOT ONLY RIPS THE LID OFF OF DARK SUBJECTS, BUT LAYS THEM AT OUR FEET IN A COMPREHENSIVE MANNER TO BE OBSERVED AND UNDERSTOOD. *CEMETERY GATES: DEATH AND MOURNING THROUGH THE AGES* IS A FASCINATING BOOK THAT SHEDS LIGHT UPON OUR FINAL INEVITABLE RITE OF PASSAGE AND OUR QUEST FOR THE PROOF OF AN AFTERLIFE. UTTERLY FASCINATING!

~ Rev. Tim Shaw
Host of the *Black Cat Lounge Radio Hour*

IT'S NOT EASY TO TAKE A SUBJECT LIKE DEATH AND TURN IT INTO A BOOK THAT IS ACTUALLY ENJOYABLE AND HARD TO PUT DOWN. *CEMETERY GATES: DEATH AND MOURNING THROUGH THE AGES* DOES JUST THAT. IT IS A FASCINATING LOOK INTO ALL ASPECTS OF DEATH FROM CROSSING OVER, TO BURIAL RITES AND CUSTOMS, THE AFTERLIFE AND EVERYTHING IN BETWEEN. IF DEATH WERE A COLOR, MOST WOULD SEE IT AS BLACK, BUT AUTHOR CORVIS NOCTURNUM PAINTS DEATH IN A COLORFUL SPECTRUM THAT IS PLEASING TO THE EYE AND THE SOUL.

~Marla Brooks, Author
Workplace Spells and *Animal Spells and Magick*

Embracing the Darkness:
Understanding Dark Subcultures

A POIGNANT AND INTROSPECTIVE VOYAGE INTO DARK SUBCULTURES WITH A HUMANISTIC APPROACH...A MUST-HAVE FOR ANYONE WHO HAS EVER WONDERED WHAT DRAWS US TO THE DARK SIDE.

~ *Dark Realms Magazine*

A Mirror Darkly

CORVIS NOCTURNUM DELVES INTO THE
DARK SIDE WITH CLARITY AND VISION.

~ Reverend Shane Bugbee
Radio Free Satan

Promethean Flame

PROMETHEAN FLAME TRACES VARIED THREADS OF FREE-THINKING
AS PRACTICED BY RAMPANT INDIVIDUALISTS, SORCERERS, ROGUES,
AND CREATORS AS WELL AS SECRET SOCIETIES, ALSO TOUCHING UPON
HOW THEIR INEXTINGUISHABLE SPARKS CONTINUE TO IMPACT OUR
CONTEMPORARY CULTURE IN BOTH CINEMA AND MUSIC. IT WILL KINDLE
YOUR DESIRE TO DELVE EVEN MORE DEEPLY INTO THESE FASCINATING
PEOPLE."

~ Magus Peter H. Gilmore
High Priest, Church of Satan

PROMETHEAN FLAME IS AN EXCELLENT STUDY INTO PARTICULAR
DEVELOPMENTS OF MAGICKAL PRACTICE AND ESOTERIC SPIRITUALITY.
WITH DETERMINATION, THE AUTHOR BLENDS WELL-RESEARCHED
INFORMATION ABOUT KEY FIGURES KNOWN FOR THEIR INVOLVEMENT
IN FREE-THINKING MAGICKAL SPIRITUALITY, AND EXAMINES OCCULT
ORDERS FROM ANCIENT TIMES TO MODERNITY, EVEN ILLUMINATING
SIGNIFICANT CONCEPTS BY LINKING HISTORICAL DETAILS TO
MODERN CINEMA! FROM JOHN DEE TO ISAAC NEWTON; FROM THE
GOLDEN DAWN TO THE ILLUMINATI; FROM ZEUS TO BAPHOMET,
PROMETHEAN FLAME DOCUMENTS A WIDE ARRAY OF HISTORY
PERTINENT TO ANYONE IMMERSING THEMSELVES IN THE MAGICKAL
ARTS, BE THEY A HERMETICIST, CEREMONIAL MAGICIAN, WITCH,
OR ESOTERICIST.

~ Raven Digitalis, Author
Goth Craft: The Magickal Side of Dark Culture

Occult researcher and Gothic fantasy artist E. R. Vernor, best known to his fans under the pen name Corvis Nocturnum, has owned an occult shop for several years while he maintained office as the Vice President of the Fort Wayne Pagan Alliance, a faith tolerance organization, and acted as Vendor Director/Coordinator for Pagan Pride Day in Fort Wayne, Indiana. He has conducted lectures at various events all over Indiana, Ohio, and Illinois on the subjects in his first book *Embracing the Darkness; Understanding Dark Subcultures*, which details the truth and crossover of alternative lifestyles, gaining the attention of readers all over the world. This grand and great-grandson of a Mason remains involved in bringing about public awareness to Goth culture, witchcraft, and Satanism's true nature at conventions and universities, by being an invited speaker at the 2006 World Religions Seminar at the Indiana-Purdue University Fort Wayne, and guest panelist for the 2010 Kheperu Open House where he enlightened the convention attendees about the

About the Author

misconceptions of Satanism. He has also been a consultant for A&E's *Paranormal States* episode "Satan's Soldier." He has been an active voice in many dark communities, promoting public awareness on various issues, such as ethics, and explaining away stereotypes as host of his own radio show, *Embrace the Dark* and as a guest of a multitude of online radio shows. The author has had appearances in magazines such as the October 2009 *Penthouse Magazine* article interview on sex and Satanism, and he occasionally is a writer for *Dark Resurrected Magazine*.

Corvis Nocturnum/E.R. Vernor is a May 2010 graduate with Presidents List Honor Roll from Brown Mackie College, with dual associates degrees in Business Management and Criminal Justice. In his free time, he enjoys oil painting works of fantasy, pagan, and Gothic artwork. He is the cofounder and publisher of Dark Moon Press, while working on new books including *Satan's Minions: A Guide to Fallen Angels, Demons and other Dark Creatures.*

Other works by author include:
Embracing the Darkness; Understanding Dark Subcultures, (Dark Moon Press, 2005)
A Mirror Darkly, (Dark Moon Press, 2006)
Promethean Flame, (Dark Moon Press, 2008)
Allure of the Vampire; Our Sexual Attraction to the Undead, (Dark Moon Press, 2009)
Cemetery Gates; Death and Mourning through the Ages (Schiffer Publishing, 2011)

Corvis Nocturnum can be reached for questions and appearances at: corvisnocturnum@yahoo.com or to written mail via P.O. Box 11496, Fort Wayne, IN 46858.

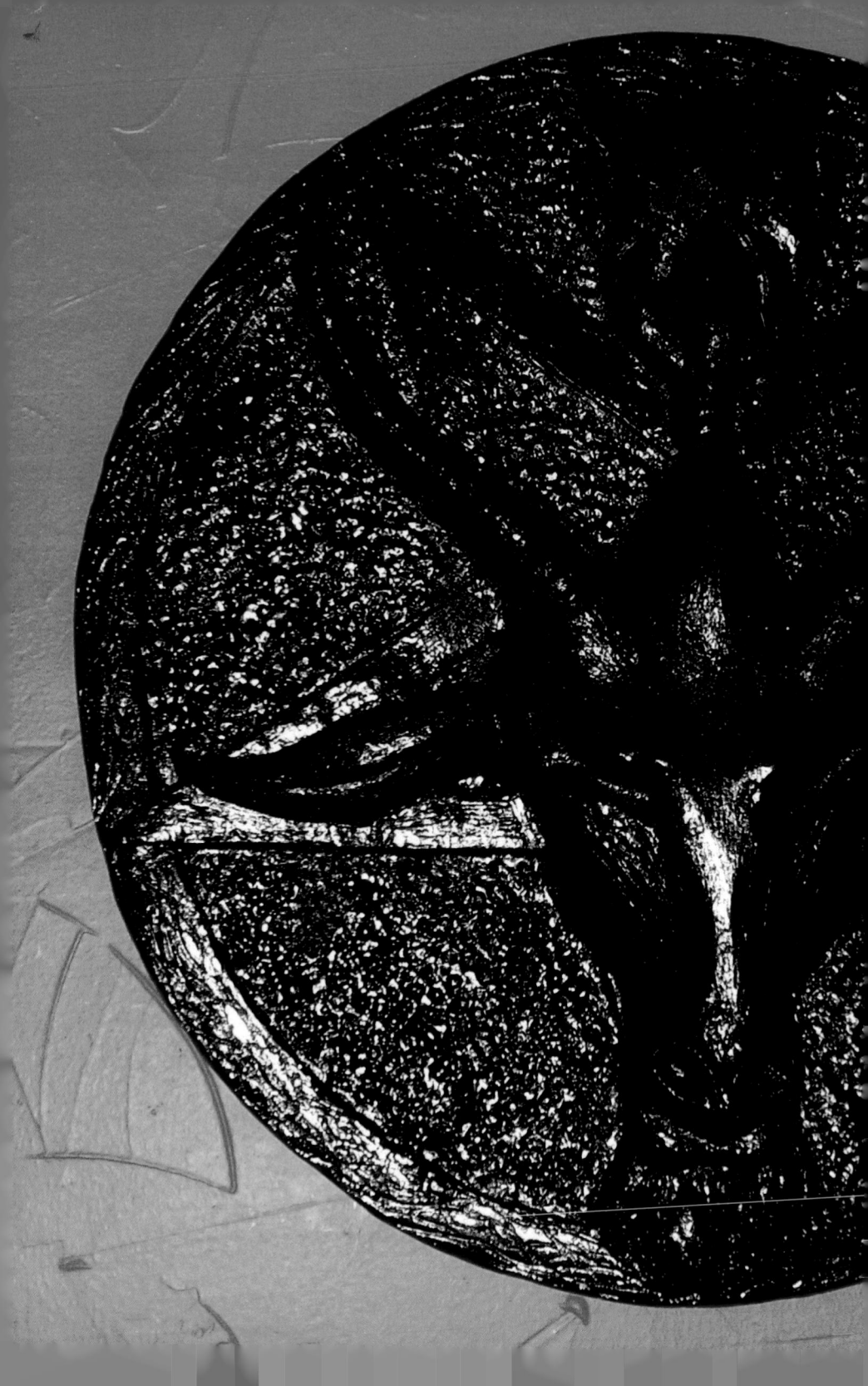